BAPTISTWAY®

## Adult Bible Teaching Guide

# The Gospel of John

*So That You May Believe*

James Cooper
Bill Pinson, Jr.
Travis Bundrick
Israel Galindo
Larry Shotwell

BAPTISTWAY PRESS®
Dallas, Texas

BAPTISTWAY PRESS® Management Team
Executive Director, Baptist General Convention of Texas: Charles Wade
Coordinator, Church Health and Growth Section: H. Lynn Eckeberger
Director, Bible Study/Discipleship Center: Dennis Parrott
Administrator, Curriculum Development: Bernard M. Spooner

Publishing consultant: Ross West, Positive Difference Communications
Cover and Interior Design and Production: Desktop Miracles, Inc.
Front Cover Photo: Scene from Galilee, BiblePlaces.com

First edition: March 2003
ISBN: 1–931060–34–7

# How to Make the Best Use of This Teaching Guide

Leading a class in studying the Bible is a sacred trust. This *Teaching Guide* has been prepared to help you as you give your best to this important task.

In each lesson, you will find first "Bible Comments" for teachers, to aid you in your study and preparation. The three sections of "Bible Comments" are "Understanding the Context," "Interpreting the Scriptures," and "Focusing on the Meaning." "Understanding the Context" provides a summary overview of the entire background passage that also sets the passage in the context of the Bible book being studied. "Interpreting the Scriptures" provides verse-by-verse comments on the focal passage. "Focusing on the Meaning" offers help with the meaning and application of the focal text.

The second main part of each lesson is "Teaching Plans." You'll find two complete teaching plans in this section. The first is called "Teaching Plan—Varied Learning Activities," and the second is called "Teaching Plan—Lecture and Questions." Choose the plan that best fits your class and your style of teaching. You may also use and adapt ideas from both. Each plan is intended to be practical, helpful, and immediately useful as you prepare to teach. The major headings in each teaching plan are intended to help you sequence how you teach so as to follow the flow of how people tend to learn. The first major heading, "Connect with Life," provides ideas that will help you begin the class session where your class is and draw your class into the study. The second major heading, "Guide Bible Study," offers suggestions for helping your class engage the Scriptures actively and develop a greater understanding of this portion of the Bible's message. The third major heading, "Encourage Application," is meant to help participants focus on how to respond with their lives to this message.

As you and your class begin the study, take time to lead them in writing the date on which each lesson will be studied on the first page of each lesson and/or on the contents page of the *Study Guide*. You may also find it helpful to make and post a chart that indicates the date on which each lesson will be studied. If all of your class has e-mail, send them an e-mail with the dates the lessons will be studied.

Here are some steps you can take to help you prepare well to teach each lesson and save time in doing so:

1. Start early in the week before your class meets.

2. Overview the study in the *Study Guide*. Look at the table of contents, read the study introduction, and read the unit introduction for the lesson you are about to study. Try to see how each lesson relates to the unit and overall study of which it is a part.

3. Consider carefully the suggested Main Idea, Question to Explore, and Teaching Aim. These can help you discover the main thrust of this particular lesson.

4. Use your Bible to read and consider prayerfully the Scripture passages for the lesson. (Each writer of the Bible comments in both the *Teaching Guide* and the *Study Guide* has chosen a favorite translation. You're free to use the Bible translation you prefer and compare it with the translations chosen, of course.)

5. After reading all the Scripture passages in your Bible, then read the Bible comments in the *Study Guide*. The Bible comments are intended to be an aid to your study of the Bible. Read also the small articles—"sidebars"—in each lesson. They are intended to provide additional, enrichment information and inspiration and to encourage thought and application. Try to answer for yourself the questions included in each lesson. They're intended to encourage further thought and application, and you can also use them in the class session itself. Continue your Bible study with the aid of the Bible comments included in this *Teaching Guide*.

6. Review the "Teaching Plans" in this *Teaching Guide*. Consider how these suggestions would help you teach this Bible passage in your class to accomplish the teaching aim.

7. Consider prayerfully the needs of your class and how to teach so you can help your class learn best.

8. Develop and follow a lesson plan based on the suggestions in this *Teaching Guide*, with alterations as needed for your class.

9. Enjoy leading your class in discovering the meaning of the Scripture passages and in applying these passages to their lives.

In addition, you may want to get the enrichment teaching help that is provided in both the printed and Internet editions of the *Baptist Standard*. Call 214–630–4571 to begin your subscription to the *Baptist Standard*. Access the internet information by checking the *Baptist Standard* website at http://www.baptiststandard.com. (Other class participants may find this information helpful, too.)

# John: So That You May Believe

*How to Make the Best Use of This Teaching Guide*            3

UNIT ONE

## The Word and His Works

**Date of Study**

LESSON 1        _____    *God in the Flesh*
                             John 1:1–18                          9

LESSON 2        _____    *Whatever Jesus Tells You*
                             John 2:1–22                         20

LESSON 3        _____    *For God So Loved*
                             John 3:1–16                         31

LESSON 4        _____    *If You Knew the Gift of God*
                             John 4:4–30, 39–42                  42

LESSON 5        _____    *The Case for Jesus*
                             John 5:1–24, 31–40                  53

UNIT TWO

## The Growing Conflict

LESSON 6        _____    *To Whom Shall We Go?*
                             John 6:41–58, 66–69                 64

LESSON 7        _____    *The Good Shepherd and Human Blindness*
                             John 9:1–7; 9:39—10:19              76

UNIT THREE

## The Time Has Come

LESSON 8        _____    *The Resurrection and the Life*
                             John 11:14–44, 47–53                87

LESSON 9        _____    *The Hour Has Come*
                             John 11:55–57; 12:20–37, 44–50      99

U N I T    F O U R

## Jesus' Glorious Triumph

LESSON 10   _____    *Do As Jesus Did*
John 13:1–17    111

LESSON 11   _____    *Never Alone*
John 14:15–27; 15:26—16:15    121

LESSON 12   _____    *"It Is Finished"*
John 19:1–21, 26–30    132

LESSON 13   _____    *Seeing and Believing*
John 20:1–2, 11–29    143

*How to Order More Bible Study Materials*    155

## Focal Text

John 1:1–18

## Background

John 1

## Main Idea

In Jesus the eternal Word became flesh, revealing God uniquely and offering those who trust in him the right to become God's children.

## Question to Explore

Who is Jesus, really?

## Teaching Aim

To help the class explain the significance for their lives of who Jesus is

## Lesson One

# God in the Flesh

## BIBLE COMMENTS

### Understanding the Context

The opening words of the Gospel of John clearly demonstrate that this gospel is different from the other three. Matthew, Mark, and Luke are termed the synoptic gospels because they each "see" the life and teachings of Jesus in a similar way. The Gospel of John does not contradict the other three, but it does look at the life and teachings of Jesus in a different way. For example, the Gospel of John focuses on aspects of Jesus' life and teachings not emphasized in the other accounts, majors on a discussion of "signs" that indicate the true nature of Jesus, links profound teachings to miracles, and deals with issues and heresies not addressed in the other three.

Who wrote this gospel? Most scholars agree that it was John the disciple of Jesus, who was the younger son of Salome and Zebedee and who was the brother of James (see Matthew 27:56; Mark 15:40). John was part of the inner circle of disciples along with Peter and James. Stories about John in his later years show him as a kind and loving person. Perhaps the most important thing about him in relation to the Gospel of John is that he knew Jesus first hand and up close. No hearsay clouds this account.

Most scholars agree that John wrote or compiled this gospel about 100 AD, although some place it earlier. By this time the Christian movement had penetrated the Greek world. John framed the gospel to deal with issues that confronted the Christian movement at this time and in this setting.

Clearly the primary focus of the Gospel of John is to answer the question, *Who is Jesus?* The first chapter furnishes numerous insights from the words and the titles used to describe Jesus both in the prologue (1:1–18) and in his relation to John the Baptist and the calling of the first disciples. These words and titles include "life," "light, "the One and Only," "the Lamb of God," "rabbi," "Messiah," "King of Israel," "Son of God," and "Son of Man." However, the answer to the question that permeates the Gospel of John is this: "The Word became flesh and made his dwelling among us" (1:14).

## Interpreting the Scriptures

### Jesus As the Word (1:1–15)

**1:1–2.** "Word" is the translation of the Greek word *logos*. The *logos* played a huge role in Greek thought. The *logos* was the mind of God that gave order to the world and reason to human beings. John used the concept of the *logos* to relate the gospel of the Lord Jesus Christ to the Greek world. He also used the word to deal with a major heresy that had developed in the Christian movement—Gnosticism.

A major aspect of much of Greek thought was that the material world was only a shadow of the real world, which was a world of ideas. From this concept the notion developed that matter was evil and spirit was good. For some so-called Christians this meant that God as spirit was good and therefore could having nothing to do with physical matter, which was evil. So how was the world created? According to this heretical view a series of emanations came from God, each further and further removed from God, until one was far enough removed to be able to touch or create physical matter. However, this god was so far removed from the true God that it had no knowledge of the true God and in fact was something of an enemy of God. This heresy tended either to picture Jesus as this semi-god of creation or as a sort of spirit or phantom that was not really human.

The prologue to the Gospel of John (1:1–18) sets out to counter this heresy as well as to relate Christian teaching to the Greek world of thought. Jesus as the Word of God was both completely divine and totally human. To counter the heresy that the Word was some sort of emanation from God, John declares: "In the beginning was the Word, and the Word was with God, and the Word was God. He was with God in the beginning."

**1:3.** In contrast to the heresy that God (as good spirit) could not touch the physical world (evil matter) John states that the Word created all things. This is the same Word that John speaks of as being God. In so doing John sets the stage for his later assertion that Jesus was God in the flesh.

**1:4.** Not only did the Word create all physical matter, but the Word also is the source of life. Thus the Word is the source of both animate and inanimate matter. Life separates human beings from inanimate objects and gives people the ability to reason. That reason should have led people to the light of understanding that God is the source of life.

**1:5.** The darkness that clouds human understanding has prevented people from knowing and relating to God. One way to translate the phrase in this verse related to the light from God is "the darkness has not understood it." Another possible translation is "the darkness has not overcome it" (see NRSV and alternate renderings in NIV and NASB). In either case, the light has not been extinguished. Jesus, as the light of the world, is still available for those who will trust and follow him.

## John the Witness (1:6–9)

**1:6.** One of the heresies in the early Christian movement gave to John the Baptist a place far above what he deserved, making him almost semi-divine. John, the author of the Gospel of John, gave John the Baptist (as he is called in the synoptic gospels) the recognition he deserved (he "was sent from God") but also fit him into the proper order of things. John the Baptist was not the light of the world; Jesus is.

**1:7–8.** Thus John the Baptist was a witness to the true nature of Jesus. As a witness his function was to testify as to what he knew to be true. The purpose of his testimony was not to garner praise to himself but that "through him all men might believe." John emphasized the fact that the Baptizer was not the light but only a witness to the light.

**1:9.** John states that Jesus was the "true" light, or perhaps better translated, the *real* light. Greek philosophers taught that the real world was the world of ideals and the physical world was only a shadow of these ideals. In Jesus the real light penetrated the darkness of our world. Before Jesus, people had glimpses of what was true or real, but in him the full glory of truth shone brightly.

Furthermore, this light was for "every man," referring to all people. Such inclusiveness contrasted with the exclusiveness of Jews, Greeks, and Romans, each of whom considered their kind better than others. Yet John sets forth the startling claim that the real light is available to everyone.

### The Word Among Us (1:10–14)

**1:10.** How was the Word in the world? The world was created and sustained by Jesus, the Word of God. The Bible indicates that people should have recognized the hand of God in creation. The psalmist stated, "The heavens declare the glory of God; / the skies proclaim the work of his hands" (Psalm 19:1). Paul, the missionary apostle, writing to the Roman Christians, asserted, "For since the creation of the world God's invisible qualities—his eternal power and divine nature—have been clearly seen, being understood from what has been made, so that men are without excuse" (Romans 1:20). Yet "the world did not recognize him" (John 1:10).

**1:11.** "His own" were the Jewish people. God had chosen the people of Israel, not for special privilege but for special responsibility. Through their history and the words of their prophets they had been prepared for the coming of the Christ. Of all peoples they should have been the ones most likely to recognize Jesus for who he really was. But "his own did not receive him."

**1:12.** Although the Jewish people were "his own," they did not have exclusive rights to be the children of God. In fact, all people who "received him" were given the right to become children of God. One of the early struggles in the Christian movement was whether a person had to become a Jew before becoming a Christian. Paul and others insisted that a person became a child of God not by works of the Jewish law but by faith in Jesus as the Son of God, the Savior of the world. The competency of each person to know God's will is evident in this passage.

**1:13.** John hammers home the truth that a person becomes a child of God not by human relationship or action but by divine will. Some Jews claimed that they were the children of God because they were born Jews. Some Greek philosophers believed that they could become god-like through reason or discipline. John counters such false views.

**1:14.** The Word had been present in the world from the beginning of creation. Now the Word has come into the world in a very special way: "The Word became flesh and made his dwelling among us." This truth blasted once and for all the idea that God could not or would not have anything to do with the physical world. It also dismissed the claim that Jesus was not fully human if he were God. In this statement rests the basic doctrine of Christ: Christ was both fully divine and completely human. Our finite minds cannot comprehend such a truth, but by faith we accept it as fact.

The "glory" of the Word that became flesh is the "glory" of God himself. As God is filled with "grace" and "truth" so is the Word made flesh. "Grace" is the unmerited love of God, the love that is extended to us through Jesus Christ. "Truth" is an attribute central to the nature of the Word. The theme of "truth" is sounded throughout the Gospel of John.

## The Witness of John the Baptist (1:15–18)

**1:15.** John the Baptist always made clear that he was in no way equal to Jesus. In this statement John the Baptist testified that although Jesus began his ministry after he, John the Baptist, began his, Jesus had surpassed him. The reason given for Jesus' supremacy likely shocked some and was incomprehensible to others. John stated that Jesus "was before me." Of course, this was true because Jesus was the Word and "in the beginning was the Word and the Word was with God, and the Word was God. . . . Through him all things were made" (1:1, 3). John the Baptist later further clarified his role in relation to that of Jesus (1:19–34; 3:25–30; see also 5:31–36).

**1:16.** "Fullness" means complete. "Grace" is unmerited love or good will. The love of Jesus is complete. From this absolutely perfect love flows blessing after blessing.

**1:17.** The law as recorded in the Old Testament was revealed to Moses. The law had a purpose in God's divine plan. It was not the final word in that plan, however. The Word made flesh—that is, Jesus—was the final word. The law brought rules and regulations, helpful but not capable of doing what Jesus brought—grace and truth.

**1:18.** Jesus could do what he did because of his absolute uniqueness. He was one with God and could reveal God in ways that no one else could. Not even Moses, who had known God in a special way, could make God known as Jesus could (see Exodus 33:20–23; Deuteronomy 34:10–12). Basically John was saying, *If you want to know what God is like, look at Jesus.* Thus, recording the life and teachings of Jesus became supremely important because for those who did not know Jesus in the flesh, as John did, having this account of Jesus was for them a way to know God.

## Focusing on the Meaning

This brief passage presents a stimulating number of awesome truths. Central to them all and to the Gospel of John itself is the fact that "the Word became flesh and made his dwelling among us" (John 1:14).

Many varied ideas existed in Jesus' day about who he was and what his purpose was. Such ideas also exist today. John's Gospel makes clear the identity and purpose of Jesus and establishes his uniqueness. In all the various religions of the world the truth is conveyed through words like these: *Let me tell you how to live.* In Christ the Word became flesh, conveying this message: *Let me show you how to live.* Jesus shows us what God is like. Furthermore, he died to set us free from the power of sin so that we could follow the way he has shown us. Also, he is alive to indwell us to provide the guidance and the power needed to follow his way.

John the Baptist was a witness, and he gave testimony concerning Jesus. Each one of us can and should be such a witness and give similar testimony. In a courtroom the witness does not function as judge or jury, determining guilt or innocence, or as an attorney, brilliantly presenting arguments. Instead the witness has one primary purpose: to testify to what he or she knows to be true because of personal experience. So it is with witnessing to the truth about Jesus. We are to testify to what we know to be true because of personal experience with him. Such testimony requires no special training but only a faith relationship with Jesus as Savior and Lord.

John the Baptist also set an example in giving all the glory to Jesus Christ. In our testimony we should be careful to glorify who Jesus is and what he has done and is doing and not ourselves.

In sharing our witness we ought to keep in mind how best to communicate the truth about Christ. The truth is timeless, but the method and words used to communicate may change according to the people to whom we testify. In writing his gospel, John did just that as he related to a Greek world in terms that would not only gain their attention but also assist their understanding.

# TEACHING PLANS

## Teaching Plan—Varied Learning Activities

### Connect with Life

1. Invite participants to open the *Study Guide* to the listing of the lessons and to write the dates for the lessons in the spaces provided. Review the four units of study. Encourage everyone to look at the introduction to the study, titled, "Introducing John: So That You May Believe." Point out the purpose of the Gospel of John in paragraph one and some reasons for studying John as suggested by New Testament scholar George Beasley-Murray in paragraph four. Also refer to the three ways of approaching the study given in paragraphs six, seven, and eight.

2. Prior to the session, write or telephone members requesting them to bring one or more symbols, pictures, or objects that represent light or life. Display these items and allow members to share thoughts about them. (An optional approach is to distribute half sheets of construction paper and ask members to tear the paper to create something representing life or light.) Make the transition into the Bible study by pointing out that the lesson for today reveals how Jesus came into the world to bring life and light.

**Guide Bible Study**

3.  Use the short article titled "Logos" in the *Study Guide* to present a brief lecture on the meaning of *Logos*.

4.  On a large sheet of paper or a marker board write on the left side, "Who Is Jesus?" Write "Who is John?" in the center and "What Does the Word's Becoming Flesh Mean?" on the right side. (Note that these are the headings of the lesson comments in the *Study Guide*.) Encourage participants to listen for descriptive words or phrases about Jesus as three previously enlisted readers present the following choral reading.

    *Voice 1:* In the beginning!

    *Voice 2:* In the beginning!

    *Voice 3:* In the beginning was the Word.

    *Voice 2:* And the Word was with God.

    *Voice 1:* And the Word was God.

    *Voice 3:* He was in the beginning with God.

    *Voice 1:* All things came into being through him, and without him not one thing came into being.

    *Voice 3:* What has come into being in him was life.

    *Voice 2:* Life!

    *Voice 1:* Life!

    *Voice 3:* And the life was the light of all people.

    *Voice 2:* Light!

    *Voice 1:* Light!

    *Voice 3:* The light shines in the darkness, and the darkness did not overcome it.

    *Voice 2:* And the Word became flesh and lived among us.

    *Voice 1:* Flesh!

    *Voice 3:* Flesh!

    *Voice 2:* And we have seen his glory.

    *Voice 1:* Glory!

    *Voice 3:* Glory!

    *Voice 2:* The glory as of a father's only son, full of grace and truth.

    *Voice 1:* Grace!

    *Voice 2:* Truth!

    *Voice 1:* Here is the Lamb of God who takes away the sin of the world.

UNIT ONE: The Word and His Works

After the reading, lead the class to identify descriptive words or phrases. List them under "Who Is Jesus?" Use the comments in the *Study Guide* and this *Teaching Guide* to clarify any ideas that need explanation.

5.  Enlist a volunteer to read aloud John 1:6–9, 15. Ask participants to listen for words or phrases answering the question "Who Is John?" List ideas under the heading. Ask everyone to scan John 1:19–36 looking for other ideas about John (John the Baptist). Discuss the ideas, providing information from the comments in the *Study Guide* and this *Teaching Guide*.

6.  Ask participants to listen for answers to "What Does the Word's Becoming Flesh Mean?" as John 1:10–13, 16–18 are read. List ideas under the heading and discuss these thoughts.

## Encourage Application

7.  Ask participants to respond to the following case study.
    Lupe and Maria live next door to you. They have been married nearly three years and have a one-year-old daughter. Neither parent attended church as children and only very rarely as adults. They were married in a civil ceremony performed by a judge. During the three years Lupe and Maria have lived next door, they have become your friends. One day while your families were visiting, Lupe asked, "Why do you go to church so often?" How could you use that question to explain the significance for your life of who Jesus is so Lupe and Maria could understand?

8.  Refer again to the representations of life and light shared by the members (see step 2). Lead a discussion based on the following questions: *How has Jesus brought you life? How has Jesus brought you light?*

## Teaching Plan—Lecture and Questions

### Connect with Life

1. Invite everyone to open the *Study Guide* and write the dates for the sessions in the spaces provided. Point out the four units of study. Ask participants to turn to the article titled "Introducing John: So That You May Believe." Read paragraph four aloud and review some reasons for studying the Gospel of John. Also call attention to three ways to approach the study in paragraphs six, seven, and eight.

2. Write the following teaching outline on the marker board or large sheet of paper:
   I. Who Is Jesus? (John 1:1–5, 14)
   II. Who Is John? (John 1:6–9, 15)
   III. What Does the Word's Becoming Flesh Mean? (John 1:10–13, 16–18)

3. Read aloud the words of one of the following songs: "Shine, Jesus, Shine"[1] or "The Light of the World Is Jesus."[2] Make the transition into the Bible study by stating that the Bible study today will help us understand who Jesus is and how Jesus brought life and light into the world.

### Guide Bible Study

4. Use the brief article titled "Logos" in the *Study Guide* to present a brief lecture on the subject. An optional approach is to enlist a person who enjoys research to prepare a three-minute report on *Logos* and present the report to the class.

5. Enlist a volunteer to read aloud John 1:1–5, 14, 29. Use information from the *Study Guide* and "Bible Comments" in this *Teaching Guide* to present a brief lecture on how these verses answer the question, "Who is Jesus?" Include ideas about how these verses indicate that Jesus was both fully divine and fully human. After the lecture ask participants to share ideas in response to questions 1 and 2 at the end of the lesson in the *Study Guide*.

6. Refer to question 3 in the *Study Guide*, and ask members to listen for answers as you read aloud John 1:6–9, 15. Refer to John 1:19–34

to discover additional ideas about John the Baptist. In a brief lecture, answer the question, "Who is John?" Allow for discussion of John the Baptist as needed.

7. Refer to point III on the outline and indicate that everyone should listen for answers to the question, "What does the Word's becoming flesh mean?" Enlist a volunteer to read aloud John 1:10–13, 16–18. Present the following ideas in a brief lecture:
   a. The coming of Jesus allowed people to become children of God.
   b. The coming of Jesus allowed people to receive grace upon grace.
   c. The coming of Jesus allowed people to understand and know God better.

## Encourage Application

8. Write *Life* on the top left side of the marker board or large sheet of paper and *Light* on the right side. Invite participants to respond with words, phrases, or symbols about life and light. List these ideas beneath the headings. Then encourage volunteers to share answers to the following questions: *How has Jesus brought you life? How has Jesus brought you light?*

9. Ask volunteers to respond to question 4 in the *Study Guide*: "What are ways in which we can witness to people about who Jesus is?"

# NOTES

1. "Shine, Jesus, Shine," words and music by Graham Kendrick, copyright © 1987 Make Way Music.

2. "The Light of the World Is Jesus," words and music by P.P. Bliss.

## Focal Text

John 2:1–22

## Background

John 2

## Main Idea

Jesus, God's Word to us, is superior to all other answers to our deepest needs.

## Question to Explore

So *why* did Jesus turn the water into wine?

## Teaching Aim

To lead the class to contrast Jesus' superiority in meeting our deepest needs to other attempted solutions

## Lesson Two

# Whatever Jesus Tells You

## BIBLE COMMENTS

### Understanding the Context

The Gospel of John plunges immediately into the public ministry of Jesus. This gospel contains no stories of Jesus' birth or childhood. If this gospel was indeed the last one written, then John likely knew of the other gospels and did not attempt to repeat what had already been recorded. His intent was to share the marvelous, miraculous ministry of Jesus in a way to help people believe in Jesus as Lord and Savior.

John in fact states clearly that his purpose was not to set forth an exhaustive biography of Jesus but rather to share key signs that revealed Jesus as the Savior of the world: "Jesus did many other miraculous signs in the presence of his disciples, which are not recorded in this book. But these are written that you may believe that Jesus is the Christ, the Son of God, and that by believing you may have life in his name" (John 20:30–31).

In the prologue of the Gospel of John, in the account of John the Baptist's testimony about Jesus, and in the call by Christ of the first disciples—all recorded in the first chapter—no doubt is left about the true nature of Jesus. From the very beginning, the author makes clear the unique nature of Jesus: both fully divine and completely human. The remainder of the book records events that demonstrate these unique qualities of Jesus. The purpose of the record is not simply to provide an interesting biography but rather to issue a call to faith in and followship of Jesus. The brilliant way in which this purpose is carried out testifies to the guidance of the Holy Spirit in the writing of the Gospel of John. These words clearly are not the result of mere human effort; they are God-breathed.

John's Gospel focuses on both wonderful miracles and provocative actions of Jesus. These are generally followed by teachings or explanations that Jesus sets forth. Quite often the gospel records reactions of people to the miracles or acts. These reactions are both negative and positive. Some people responded by belief in Jesus. Others responded by not only reject-ing him but also desiring to eliminate him.

The two accounts in this lesson illustrate both kinds of responses. They also contrast the sufficiency and superiority of Jesus to the failure and inadequacy of Jewish rites and of the most sacred site of Judaism, the temple.

## Interpreting the Scriptures

### Jesus Meets Needs (2:1–11)

**2:1–2.** The Gospels of Matthew and Luke record the fact that Jesus grew up in Nazareth, a town in Galilee (Matthew 2:19–23; Luke 2:39–40; 4:16). Until beginning his public ministry at the age of thirty, Jesus remained at home helping his mother, who evidently had been widowed. As was Nazareth, Cana was in Galilee, and evidently Mary and Jesus were friends of the family celebrating a wedding. The fact that Mary and Jesus were invited to the wedding demonstrates that they were involved in the social life of the area. Jesus was no ascetic recluse as was John the Baptist. He was a welcomed guest at social events. When he began to gather his disciples, they too joined him in these events.

**2:3.** Wine was a traditional part of Jewish wedding feasts. For a host to run out of wine at a wedding feast would be embarrassing and even humiliating. Mary's comment to Jesus, "They have no more wine," was not merely a statement of fact but rather was an appeal: do something to help.

**2:4.** Some translations make Jesus' response to his mother sound harsh. The translation "dear woman" is more accurate. His reply has puzzled readers through the centuries. What did he mean by "My time has not yet come"? From the very beginning of his ministry Jesus knew that he ultimately would be put to death for the sins of the world. This reference to "my time" likely related to that (see also 7:30; 8:20; 12:23, 27; 13:1; 17:1).

**2:5.** Mary had such faith in Jesus doing something to help the host out of a humiliating situation that she told the servants to do whatever Jesus told them to do. Apparently Mary was not only a friend of the family but highly respected by the servants.

**2:6.** For the benefit of both Jewish and non-Jewish readers, John explains that the water in the jars at the wedding was for ceremonial washing. The water would have been used to wash the feet of guests and then made available to the guests for the ceremonial washing of hands prior to eating. These were large pots holding "twenty to thirty gallons" each.

**2:7.** Apparently the host had not only run out of wine but also out of water. The pots seem to have been empty. When Jesus told the servants to fill the pots with water they may have made no connection with the problem caused by the exhausted wine supply. They may have thought that simply more water was needed.

**2:8.** When did the water turn to wine? Was it when the pots were filled? when the servants took some of the liquid to the master of ceremonies? when the master of the feast drank the liquid? We do not know, but we do know that the water was turned to wine by Jesus. We also know that Jesus involved others in the miracle—the servants and the master of the feast.

**2:9–10.** The master of the feast did not know the source of the wine but upon tasting it realized that it was better than what had been served before, likely better than any he had ever tasted. In this act Jesus was indicating the old wine of the law was being replaced by something new and better: grace. The miracle not only displayed Jesus' power over the physical world but also his superiority to the rites and traditions of Judaism.

**2:11.** The master of the feast and perhaps the guests did not know the source of the marvelous beverage. The servants knew. Apparently the disciples also knew because the miraculous act helped the disciples to "put their faith in him." The first of Jesus' "miraculous signs" was done in an out-of-the-way place. John's Gospel records many of the "signs" of Jesus, miraculous acts that demonstrate who he was and what he had come to do.

## Jesus Cleanses the Temple (2:12–22)

**2:12.** The most likely site for Capernaum is on the north shore of the Sea of Galilee. Cana may have been in the highlands of Galilee. Thus the gospel indicates that Jesus went "down" to Capernaum. We do not know why Jesus went to Capernaum. However, John does not record events unimportant to his purpose. Jesus may have paused in Capernaum as a sort of retreat, realizing that as he journeyed to Jerusalem he would confront hostility as he carried out his mission. Even Jesus withdrew from time to time for renewal.

**2:13.** The Jewish Passover was a major event. Held in the spring of the year, Passover was a celebration of the time when the death angel passed over the children of Israel in bondage in Egypt (see Exodus 12). Every Jewish male living within twenty miles of Jerusalem was required to attend (see Deuteronomy 16:16). Others journeyed from distant places to participate.

Jerusalem is located south of Galilee. We usually speak of going "down" when we go south and "up" when we go north. However, because of the prominence of Jerusalem the biblical writers always speak of going "up" to Jerusalem.

The other gospels record only one visit by Jesus to Jerusalem, other than his journey there as a child. John records several. Is there a conflict in the accounts? No. Remember that John's Gospel does not contradict but rather complements or supplements the other Gospels. He records a number of events not mentioned by the other chroniclers of Jesus' life and teachings. Matthew, Mark, and Luke major on Jesus' ministry in Galilee; John focuses on his ministry in and around Jerusalem.

A chronological difference exists, however, in the account of John and that of the other three gospels as to when the cleansing of the temple occurred. John puts this event at the beginning of Jesus' ministry and the other three at the end. Through the centuries, scholars have speculated about this difference. No agreement has been reached as to why the difference exists. Jesus may have cleansed the temple twice. If only once, John may have placed the account here in his narrative to emphasize the fact that Jesus fulfilled Messianic prophecy concerning the temple (see Malachi 3:1–4, for example). As we have noted, John was up front with a full disclosure of who Jesus was and what he had come to do.

**2:14.** The sight that greeted Jesus when he entered the courts of the temple moved him to radical action. Why? Because greed and injustice were rampant, all in the name of religion—in the name of God. Here was the situation. Jews came to the Passover Feast from many places, some from very distant countries. Many were poor and journeyed at considerable sacrifice. To worship in the temple a person had to pay a temple tax. The money was used to operate the sacrificial system of the temple. Only certain coins were acceptable to pay the tax. People coming from many different places brought a variety of currencies with them. In order to pay the tax a person had to exchange this currency for the coins acceptable for the temple tax. The moneychangers charged an exorbitant amount to change the money. Thus poor pilgrims were forced to pay crippling sums in order to worship, and the temple authorities allowed this practice to flourish.

Furthermore, people worshipping in the temple often desired to make a sacrifice. If they had traveled long distances, they could not bring a sacrifice with them, such as a lamb or even a dove. The people selling sacrificial animals in the temple courts charged astronomical sums. If a person chose to purchase an animal outside the temple courts, these were subject to inspection by the temple authorities because only perfect animals, according to the Jewish law, could be offered as sacrifice. Inevitably the inspectors would refuse to approve an animal purchased outside of the temple, thus forcing a person to buy one inside at the exaggerated price. Jesus refused to tolerate a system that took advantage of the poor in this unscrupulous fashion in the name of religion.

**2:15–16.** Jesus reacted to the sacrilege by making a whip from the cords used to bind the animals and clearing the area of such unscrupulous activity. Picture the scene: tables overturned and money scattered, men and beasts running, and Jesus shouting, "Get these out of here!" His actions not only were aimed at correcting injustices but also at challenging the system of temple worship itself.

**2:17.** Viewing Jesus' deep feelings, the disciples remembered Psalm 69:9. They seem to have regarded this event as pointing to Jesus' being the Messiah.

**2:18.** The Jews in the temple, likely the Jewish authorities, saw no such sign in Jesus' actions. Instead they demanded a miraculous sign of his authority to carry out such cleansing.

**2:19–20.** Jesus told them that the sign of his authority was that when the "temple" was destroyed he would restore it in three days. The Jews thought he was speaking of the temple building and scorned Jesus' reply. They said that it had taken forty-six years to build the temple and it was ridiculous to think Jesus could build it in three days.

**2:21.** Jesus, however, was not speaking of the temple building but of his body. The sign to which he referred was the greatest sign of all: his death and resurrection.

**2:22.** Apparently the disciples did not comprehend Jesus' statement at the time. Nevertheless, after his death and resurrection they understood, and this incident helped confirm their belief in Jesus.

## Focusing on the Meaning

John presents Jesus as the one who is able to meet our needs, regardless of their nature, in a way no other person or thing can do. In the account of Jesus' visit to Cana the need he met for adequate refreshment may seem small to us, but the lack of wine would have robbed the event of joy and humiliated the host. In love, Jesus met the need. In the account of his visit to the temple the need for honesty and true worship seemed almost overwhelming, but Jesus tackled the task with vigor.

The accounts recorded by John are historical and factual. They are not parables told to convey some particular truth. Nevertheless they are "signs." In John's Gospel signs are miracles or astounding events that are historical and also demonstrate some truth about Jesus. Such is the case with these two accounts.

At Cana the sign of turning water to wine showed the concern of Jesus to bring joy into all circumstances of life. It also pointed to the fact that Jesus was the new wine of joy and grace that would replace the old wine of duty and legalism (see Matthew 9:17).

In Jerusalem at the temple the sign of driving out the sellers of sacrifice and the changers of money showed the concern of Jesus for justice. It also pointed to the fact that Jesus had come to replace the old religion of ritual and animal sacrifice in the temple with a new way of faith that could be followed anywhere. Although he was accused of saying that he would destroy the temple, he did not say this. However, by his life, death, and resurrection, Jesus did indeed make unnecessary the temple and the ritual and sacrifice that took place there.

Wherever there is need to be met, whether on a small, personal dimension such as at Cana or on a vast, public scale such as at Jerusalem, Jesus is superior to any other would-be meeter of needs. While in the flesh, Jesus was limited by space and time. However, following the resurrection he fulfills his promise to be with us always in all ways and in all places.

# TEACHING PLANS

## Teaching Plan—Varied Learning Activities

### Connect with Life

1. Encourage volunteers to share some strange or funny happenings that have occurred during weddings or at church events. Be prepared to tell something yourself to get them started, if needed. Limit the sharing to two or three brief stories. Make the transition into the Bible study by saying that this lesson deals with two events in the life of Jesus—one at a wedding and the other in the temple.

### Guide Bible Study

2. In advance, enlist a member to research and present a three-minute report on the "Signs in John's Gospel." (Refer the member to the small article "Miracles in John's Gospel" in lesson six in the *Study Guide.*) After the report, point out that John 2:11 indicates the miracle of the water being turned to wine is the first sign.

3. Distribute the "Discussion Guide." Read the Scripture passage aloud, lead discussion on each point, and encourage participants to mark the best answer as each point is discussed rather than completing the entire guide in advance. More than one answer could be correct, but encourage everyone to select what he or she thinks is the best answer. Use the responses as a way to guide discussion after the Bible verses are read.

## Discussion Guide—John 2

### Jesus Turns Water into Wine

John 2:1–2. Jesus attended the wedding in Cana because
_____ he and his disciples were invited.
_____ he enjoyed being a part of social events.
_____ he was kin to the groom.
_____ he needed to find a good place to do a miracle.

John 2:3. Mary asked Jesus to help solve the problem of running out of wine because
_____ she thought Jesus could help.
_____ she was accustomed to asking Jesus for help since Joseph was dead.
_____ she did not want the family to be embarrassed.

John 2:4–5. Jesus' response to his mother was
_____ rude.
_____ an idiomatic expression of the day.
_____ a way of declaring his independence from his mother.

John 2:6. The six water pots might have been
_____ all the pots the family owned.
_____ symbolic of the incompleteness of Judaism.

John 2:7–8. The water turned to wine when
_____ it was in the water pots.
_____ it was drawn out of the water pots.
_____ it was drawn out of the same well from which the water in the pots came.

John 2:9–11. The quantity and quality of the wine indicated that
_____ the wedding celebration was going to be the best party ever.
_____ Jesus was the Messiah and was revealing his glory.
_____ Jesus could meet the needs of people.

### Jesus Turns Over the Tables in the Temple

John 2:13–14. The primary reason Jesus cleansed the temple was
_____ the merchants and money-changers were inside the Court of the Gentiles.
_____ the merchants were taking advantage of people to make money.
_____ he was challenging the system of temple worship.

John 2:15–17. Jesus' actions of driving out the money-changers and the animals and overturning the tables showed that Jesus was
_____ not in control of his emotions.
_____ not pleased with the entire sacrificial system.
_____ suggesting that nothing should ever be sold in a church building.

John 2:18–22. The response of Jesus to the Jewish leaders that he would rebuild the temple in three days
_____ was not understood until Jesus was raised from the dead.
_____ indicates that Jesus would become the new temple of God.
_____ was understood by the Jewish leaders as referring to the literal temple.

## Encourage Application

4. On a marker board write *Ways Secular People Attempt to Solve Their Needs.* Ask participants to suggest ways some people attempt to solve their needs in a secular society. (Suggestions might include money, other people, business institutions, governmental institutions, self-made plans, etc.)

5. Invite volunteers to share reasons depending on Jesus to help meet their deepest needs is superior to other solutions, giving examples how their needs have been met.

6. Invite everyone to spend a moment in silent prayer asking God to help with a problem or need that is being faced at this time. Close with a brief prayer.

## Teaching Plan—Lecture and Questions

### Connect with Life

1. Tell the following story or a humorous experience of your own:

   A small boy was asked to serve as a ring-bearer at a wedding. He was proud of his opportunity to be a part of such a big event. He felt his importance as he participated in the rehearsal, wore his rented tuxedo, and walked down the aisle carrying his pillow with rings on top. He took his place near the groom and his attendants and waited for the cue to provide the rings. When the time came for the ring ceremony, the pastor took the real rings from the best man instead of using the fake rings attached to the pillow. The boy yelled out, "What about mine?" Attendants nearby tried to explain softly to him that his rings were fake. He said loudly, "I quit," threw his pillow in the air, walked off the platform, and ran to his embarrassed parents.

   Make the transition into the lesson by saying that funny things happen at weddings, and that the lesson for today involves two events in the life of Jesus where interesting and strange things happened at a wedding and at the temple.

## Guide Bible Study

2. In advance make a poster like the following:

> ### The "Signs" of John's Gospel
> Turning Water into Wine (2:1–11)
> Healing the Officer's Son (4:46–54)
> Curing a Lame Man (5:1–9)
> Feeding the Five Thousand (6:1–15)
> Walking on the Water (6:16–21)
> Restoring Sight to a Man Born Blind (9:1–7)
> Raising Lazarus from the Dead (11:1–44)

Refer to the poster and present a brief lecture on the signs in John's Gospel. Refer as seems helpful to the small article, "Miracles in John's Gospel," in lesson six in the *Study Guide*. Note that these miracles point to Jesus as Messiah and the fulfillment of Jewish religious expectations. Ask participants to respond to questions 1 and 2 in the *Study Guide*.

3. Enlist a volunteer to read John 2:1–10 aloud. Write the following points on the left side of a marker board as you present information on each from the *Study Guide* and "Bible Comments" on these verses in this *Teaching Guide*:
   (1) The participation of Jesus in social events
   (2) The importance of plenty of food and drink at a wedding feast
   (3) Mary's request of Jesus and his response
   (4) The significance of the six water pots
   (5) The quantity and quality of the wine

   After the lecture ask, *How does John 2:11 help us understand the significance and meaning of this miraculous sign?* Then ask question 3 from the *Study Guide*.

4. Invite a volunteer to read John 2:13–22 aloud. Write the following points on the right side of a marker board as you present information on them from the *Study Guide* and "Bible Comments" on these verses in this *Teaching Guide*:

    (1) Reasons sacrificial animals were sold and money was exchanged

    (2) Reasons Jesus cleansed the temple

    (3) The meaning of Jesus' response to the Jewish leaders

## Encourage Application

5. Lead the class to suggest ways secular people attempt to meet their deepest needs. After several responses, ask them how these two events in the life of Jesus show that Jesus meets needs.

6. Share a time in your life when the way God helped you was superior to any human solution. Ask volunteers to share testimonies of God meeting their needs.

7. Distribute a 3" x 5" card to each person. Tell the class that what they write will be for their eyes only. Ask everyone to write on the card a personal need and place the card in a private location. Encourage members to pray to God to help solve their needs during the coming week. Close with prayer.

## Focal Text

John 3:1–16

## Background

John 3:1–21

## Main Idea

In love and through Jesus, God offers eternal life to those willing for God to create them anew.

## Question to Explore

How can anyone be born after having grown old?

## Teaching Aim

To lead class participants to decide whether and to what extent they are willing for God to create them anew

# UNIT ONE

**The Word and His Works**

# Lesson Three

# For God So Loved

## BIBLE COMMENTS

### Understanding the Context

Through the prologue (John 1:1–18) and the accounts of the early miracles and astounding activities of Jesus—termed "signs" by John—the Gospel of John has clearly set forth who Jesus is. Now the author sets out to expand on these ideas with a special emphasis on how Jesus brings salvation to people.

One literary tool used effectively by John is dialogue between Jesus and another person. These dialogues provide some of the most insightful passages in John's Gospel about the unique role Jesus plays in bringing salvation to lost humankind. Only John's Gospel records some of these, such as the account of the conversation between Jesus and Nicodemus.

These various dialogues reveal the inclusive nature of Jesus' ministry. On one hand he visited with Nicodemus, an elite member of society. On the other he conversed with a Samaritan woman of no social standing (4:4–12). In each case the truths about Jesus are both simple and profound, simple enough for a child to understand and yet profound enough for scholars to explore for centuries.

Since these conversations, such as that with Nicodemus, take place in private between Jesus

31

and one other person, how did John know the content of the dialogue in order to record it? We can only speculate how he knew. Perhaps Jesus told the disciples about the encounter as they visited and journeyed together. John as one of the disciples who was almost always with Jesus could have learned of the content of the conversation with Nicodemus in that way. Or Nicodemus may have told about his conversation with Jesus; Nicodemus became a follower of Jesus and likely would have recounted this conversation often. Or the Holy Spirit may have revealed it to John as he wrote. One thing is for certain: the dialogue between Jesus and Nicodemus is not only factual but one of the most significant in all the Bible.

The content of the conversation is so well-known by Christians that a danger exists that a person is likely not to search for insight, saying, *I know all about that story.* Regardless of how often a person has read the account or heard it taught, new truth awaits the prayerful, thoughtful student. Indeed, here is the heart of the good news about Jesus.

## Interpreting the Scriptures

### The Visit of Nicodemus (3:1–2)

**3:1.** A great many facts are known about Nicodemus. He was a Pharisee. The name Pharisee means *the separated one*, and the term fit the Pharisees. They dedicated themselves to fulfilling every requirement of the Old Testament law and the various interpretations of the law. The scribes set forth the requirements, the experts in the law helped to interpret these requirements, and the Pharisees swore to obey. Pharisees were not numerous in Jesus' time, but they were very influential.

Nicodemus was a member of the Jewish ruling council, the Sanhedrin. The Sanhedrin, composed of seventy men, formed the high court of Judaism. Although the conquering Romans had restricted the power of the Sanhedrin somewhat, this body still wielded vast power. The group was charged with overseeing the purity of the Jewish faith. As such, these men ferreted out heresy and sought to determine who was a true prophet and who was a false one.

**3:2.** That a person of Nicodemus's standing would come to visit a wandering, controversial, poor teacher from Galilee is amazing. In the eyes of

the world and perhaps even in the opinion of Nicodemu
beneath him in almost every way. Jesus was poor; Nic
wealthy. Jesus was not a Pharisee; Nicodemus was and thu
ered more religious than Jesus, at least more orthodox. Jesu
cial position; Nicodemus was a member of the highest rel
the Jews. Nicodemus's presence indicated the magnetis
attraction for all kinds of people.

Why did Nicodemus come to Jesus by night? He m
the meeting to be kept secret because of the controve
Jesus. He may not have wanted anyone to know he was seeking insight
from someone of Jesus' standing in society. However, Nicodemus' noc-
turnal visit may not have been the result of cowardice. He may have
wanted a private meeting so he could have Jesus all to himself without
interruption.

Nicodemus addressed Jesus with respect, calling him "Rabbi." A rabbi
was a teacher who was regarded as having great knowledge and insight.
The respect that Nicodemus had for Jesus sprang from Jesus' "miraculous
signs." Nicodemus was convinced that these could only be the work of
God. Some critics of Jesus claimed he did these miracles with the power
of Satan. Nicodemus did not share this view. Keep in mind, however, that
at this stage in their relationship, Nicodemus regarded Jesus as a marvelous teacher with God-given power but not as the Son of God, the
Savior of the world.

## The New Birth (3:3–8)

**3:3.** Sensing that Nicodemus was a genuine seeker for truth about how
to be rightly related to God, Jesus got right to the point: "No one can see
the kingdom of God unless he is born again." Regardless of how hard a
person tries, no one can live in total obedience to the will of God.
Nicodemus knew that. He had tried through ritual, morality, and obedience to the law to find peace with God but had failed.

Jesus provided the answer about how to "see the kingdom of God": be
"born again" or from above. The word translated "again" in the Greek,
the language of the New Testament, is *anothen*. The major meanings of
the word are (1) *again* in the sense of for a second time and (2) *from
above*. Both of these concepts are contained in Jesus' statement to
Nicodemus. Unless we are completely changed in the sense of being
born again by the power of God, there is no way to have the relation
with God that we need.

**3:4.** Nicodemus applied a spiritual truth to a physical process, and the result was misunderstanding. That Nicodemus would seem without understanding about the concept of being born again is strange. Both Jewish and other religions of the first-century world spoke of being born again, of making a new start.

**3:5.** Various interpretations have been given to this verse. Some erroneously take the word "water" to mean baptism. Baptism is a beautiful symbol that a person has been born again, but it is not a means to new birth. Others ascribe "water" to physical birth as when a woman's "water bursts" in the process of a baby being born. Thus Jesus could mean that a person must not only be born physically but also spiritually to enter the kingdom of God. However, the most likely interpretation is that by "water" Jesus meant cleansing and by "Spirit" Jesus meant power. Ezekiel 36:24–27 would have been the background for such an understanding and would have been well-known to Nicodemus. In Jesus a person is cleansed of past sin and empowered to overcome future sin. Thus equipped, a person is literally a new person, born again.

**3:6.** Some scholars take this verse to give credence to the interpretation of the previous verse that "water" refers to physical birth ("flesh gives birth to flesh") and "Spirit" refers to spiritual rebirth. However, this verse can also mean that those who are born only of the flesh can only live in the power of the flesh and are thus doomed to failure in an effort to live as citizens of the kingdom of God. On the other hand, those born both of the flesh and of the Spirit have the power to live as citizens of the kingdom.

**3:7–8.** Jesus told Nicodemus that he should not be surprised by the concept of a new birth from God because such a concept is found in the Hebrew Scriptures with which Nicodemus must have been thoroughly familiar. Ezekiel, for example, contains references to a new heart and a new spirit (Ezek.18:31; 36:24–27).

Jesus used the example of the wind to illustrate the concept of being born again. The word in both Hebrew and Greek for spirit also means wind. Jesus pointed out that the wind is a mystery. The wind cannot be seen, and it comes and goes "wherever it pleases." Yet the wind is evident by its sound and effect. So with the Spirit: the work of the Spirit is a mystery, not able to be understood or fully explained, but the effect of the Spirit in human life is evident. You can tell whether a person has been born of the Spirit by the evidence in his or her life.

## The Way to Eternal Life (3:9–16)

**3:9–12.** Nicodemus continued to fail to comprehend what Jesus was saying. Jesus expressed frustration that a person of such knowledge of the Scriptures should be so blind to the truth as not to understand. Jesus indicated that if Nicodemus could not understand when Jesus had used simple illustrations from everyday life he would not be able to understand the truly deep truths of God.

**3:13.** Some biblical scholars believe that this verse is a comment by John rather than the words of Jesus. Their reason for this is that the words seem to be a sort of commentary on the resurrection and ascension of Jesus after the fact. The verse states that Jesus, the Son of Man, was the only one who had come from heaven and returned to heaven. However, the words could certainly be those of Jesus himself, for he sometimes spoke of his death, resurrection, and ascension in ways that were understood fully only after these occurred. Jesus' statement concerning the temple being destroyed and rebuilt in three days is an example of this (2:19).

**3:14.** Jesus used an account out of the Old Testament, Numbers 21:4–9, to share a major truth. When the Hebrew people escaped Egypt under the leadership of Moses they were not always happy with their circumstances. On one occasion when they were murmuring and complaining about having left Egypt, God sent a plague of fiery serpents. The people regretted their attitude and cried for mercy. God instructed Moses to erect an image of a serpent and to hold it up. Those who looked on the brazen serpent were healed and saved. In a similar but far greater way Jesus, the Son of Man, was to be lifted up. He referred, of course, to his crucifixion on a Roman cross.

**3:15.** The Hebrews who looked on the serpent were saved from physical death. People who look to Jesus and believe in him as Savior and Lord are saved from sin and death and receive eternal life.

**3:16.** This may be the most memorized verse in the Bible, likely because it contains the gospel in summary fashion. Entire volumes have been written about this one passage of Scripture. "Eternal" is the word used, which is more than merely *everlasting*. The life Jesus provides is not merely about enduring forever but emphasizes also the quality of that life. Everlasting life apart from God's love and the peace and joy that God provides in Christ would not be heaven but hell.

Note in this portion of John's Gospel the various expressions for the experience of salvation: "see the kingdom of God" (3:3); "born again" (3:3, 7); "enter the kingdom of God" (3:5); "born of water and the Spirit" (3:5); "born of the Spirit" (3:8); "have eternal life" (3:15, 16).

## Focusing on the Meaning

The account of Nicodemus's meeting with Jesus is about spiritual salvation. The coverage of the salvation is amazing. References to "the world" and "whoever" indicate that it is available to all people (3:16). The completeness of the salvation is amazing: "shall not perish but have eternal life." The cost of the salvation is amazing. It cost God sending his "one and only Son" (3:16) to suffer abuse and death, and it cost Jesus, the sinless Son of God, taking on himself our sins and paying the price for our rebellion against God. Perhaps most amazing of all, it costs those who receive this salvation nothing in the usual sense of what people might expect to pay for salvation, such as money, ritual, self-punishment, or good works. Yet like all gifts the gift of God in Christ must be accepted to be appropriated. We accept the gift by belief "in him" (3:16). As the following verses indicate, those who do not believe do not receive this salvation but condemn themselves to eternal darkness (3:18–20).

God's love stands as the stack pole of all that Jesus said. Often people think of God only in terms of wrath, judgment, condemnation, and punishment for sin. Of course those qualities are part of God's nature. Jesus, though, indicated that love was central in God's relationship with humankind. The extent of God's love for lost humanity is seen in his sending his only Son to pay the price for our salvation.

The account of Nicodemus's visit also hammers home the fact that the provision of salvation out of God's love is not something merely to be discussed but rather to be experienced. Although the Jewish leader may have been sincere in seeking truth, he seemed to lapse into needless questions. Such is frequently the case with people today. They had rather discuss theology than live it out. Thus this passage of Scripture calls for decision. The truth presented calls for response.

In sharing spiritual truth we can all learn from Jesus' example. He couched the truth of the deep things of God in simple illustrations that can be easily understood. For example, he indicated to Nicodemus that understanding exactly how spiritual rebirth occurs is not necessary in order to experience it any more than complete understanding of the wind is necessary to experience it. The proof of the reality of salvation in Christ is the change of life that belief in him brings.

# TEACHING PLANS

## Teaching Plan—Varied Learning Activities

### Connect with Life

1.  Ask volunteers to tell about a time when they had a conversation with an important or famous person. After two or three people have shared, make the transition into the Bible study by indicating that this lesson is about a conversation between two important people, Nicodemus and Jesus.

### Guide Bible Study

2.  Display a poster with the following information:

> **Who Was Nicodemus?**
>
> A Pharisee
> A Leader of the Jews
> A Man of Wealth

Read John 3:1 aloud. Refer to the outline on the poster to present a brief lecture identifying Nicodemus. Use the comments in the *Study Guide* (see short article, "Pharisee") and the *Teaching Guide*. Refer to John 19:39, indicating that Nicodemus brought a large amount of myrrh and aloes to be used in the burial of Jesus. Note that only a wealthy person would be able to bring large portions of these expensive items.

3.  Read John 3:2 aloud and ask the class to suggest reasons Nicodemus might have come to Jesus by night. After several reasons have been

suggested, indicate that no one really knows why he came by night. Suggest that for this lesson the class will "play like" Nicodemus came as a representative from the Sanhedrin. Invite the class to suppose the Sanhedrin wanted someone to talk directly to Jesus and to bring a report to them. Nicodemus came at night because that was the best time he and Jesus could get together for a private conversation.

4. In advance, enlist a person to present a report from Nicodemus to the Sanhedrin using John 3:2–10 as a basis for the report. The person playing Nicodemus could bring a self-planned report or use the monologue, "The Report of Nicodemus to the Sanhedrin." Ask the class to play the role of members of the Sanhedrin and think of questions they would like to ask Nicodemus about his encounter with Jesus.

---

### The Report of Nicodemus to the Sanhedrin

Last night I talked with this rabbi named Jesus. We know that he hasn't had the formal training of a rabbi, but he certainly is a great teacher whom God has sent to us. Also, his ability to do miracles is remarkable. He didn't respond to my efforts at complimenting his accomplishments but immediately told me I had to be born from above before I could see the kingdom of God. I thought at first he meant I had to be born again in a physical sense. I told him how absurd that was. It was funny thinking about a grown man being returned to his mother's womb.

Jesus explained that he was talking about people having a spiritual birth much like everyone had a physical birth. I sensed that he isn't concerned with our kind of religious practices, trying to keep all the rules. Instead he wants people to be changed from the inside out.

He knew I didn't understand how this could happen without keeping the law. About that time, we felt a gentle breeze. Jesus used the breeze to explain that God's Spirit was like that—we didn't know where it came from or where it went. I told him that I didn't understand how God's Spirit could change us. He said that I should understand since I was a rabbi.

Frankly, I left upset, disturbed, and bewildered. On the other hand, I really would like to feel the wind of God's Spirit come over me and free me from the burdens of trying to keep all the rules.

---

After the report, encourage the class to ask questions they think the Sanhedrin would have asked Nicodemus. Allow the person playing Nicodemus to respond to the questions. Assist with answers as needed.

5. Enlist a volunteer to read John 3:11–15 aloud. Encourage the class to respond to the following questions (see the *Study Guide* on these verses as needed):
   • Why do people today not follow Christ even after they have heard the gospel?
   • What is the significance of the term "Son of Man"?
   • How does the story of the serpent clarify what Jesus did on the cross?
   • What is the meaning of eternal life?

6. Ask everyone to read or quote John 3:16 and to respond to the following questions:
   (1) What did God do? (loved and gave)
   (2) For whom did God do it? (the world, and whoever)
   (3) Whom did God send? (one and only unique Son)
   (4) What is the needed response? (commit one's life to Jesus)
   (5) What is the result of following Jesus? (not perish, have eternal life)

## Encourage Application

7. Group participants into huddles of three or four. Encourage volunteers in the groups to share how they came to know about Jesus and how and when they initially felt their faith in him resulted in being created anew. Also suggest that after they have shared about the initial experience that they consider the extent to which they are continuing to allow Jesus to create them anew. After a time of discussion suggest that anyone who would like to talk about making a decision to follow Christ remain after class to discuss the matter. Lead the class in prayer that everyone would either accept the free gift of salvation or continue to become a more Christlike disciple.

# Teaching Plan—Lecture and Questions

## Connect with Life

1. Point out that when Jimmy Carter was President of the United States, many people across the nation talked about his claim to being a "born again" Christian. Some people were happy about his claim, but others were negative. Ask the class why some people feel negative about the term "born again." After several responses, make the transition into the Bible study by indicating that this lesson will clarify what Jesus wanted to happen to people who become his followers.

## Guide Bible Study

2. At the top of a marker board write *Lessons to Learn*. On the left side of the board write *From the Conversation*, and on the right side write *From the Sermon*. Ask a class member who is good at printing to jot down ideas under the headings as the class studies John 3:1–10 and John 3:11–16.

3. Enlist three good readers to read the parts of Nicodemus, Jesus, and the narration in 3:1–10. After the reading, present a lecture on the passage using comments in the *Study Guide* and this *Teaching Guide*. Consider the following suggested lessons to be learned from the conversation. Add any other lessons you or the class suggests.
   - Wise, moral leaders still need to come to Jesus.
   - Any time is a good time to encounter Jesus.
   - Everyone needs to be born from above.
   - Spiritual rebirth is available to everyone.
   - Not even religious leaders have all the answers.

4. Enlist a volunteer to read John 3:11–16 aloud. Lecture on this passage, considering these lessons:
   - Jesus brings first-hand knowledge of God.
   - All who commit themselves to Jesus have eternal life.
   - God loves the whole world and each individual.
   - God sent his one and only unique Son.
   - Followers of Jesus will not perish but have eternal life.

## Encourage Application

5.  Lead the class to discuss the questions near the end of the lesson in the *Study Guide.*

6.  Invite volunteers to share testimonies of how and when they learned about Jesus and when their faith in him resulted in being created anew. After this, invite testimonies also of how they continue to experience God's creating them anew. Invite anyone who has not experienced salvation to remain to talk about making such a commitment. Close with prayer that everyone will either decide to establish a relationship with Christ or will grow in his or her relationship with him.

### Focal Text

John 4:4–30, 39–42

### Background

John 4:1–42

### Main Idea

Jesus crosses all human barriers to invite all people into intimate relationship with God and with one another.

### Question to Explore

What's keeping you from Jesus—or from telling others about him?

### Teaching Aim

To lead the class to decide on ways they will follow Jesus' example in crossing the human barriers that separate people from God and one another

**U N I T   O N E**

*The Word and His Works*

## Lesson Four

# If You Knew the Gift of God

## BIBLE COMMENTS

### Understanding the Context

John's Gospel makes very clear the relationship of John the Baptist and Jesus. Since their ministries initially took place at the same time and in the same vicinity some might have thought they were in competition. John the Baptist emphatically denied any competition and in fact emphasized he was not even in the same category as Jesus. So that his own followers would not be angered by Jesus' increased following, John stated that Jesus must increase and he must decrease.

Perhaps a comparison of John with Jesus was inevitable. After all, they were both baptizing people (John 4:1–2). Apparently in order to avoid a needless discussion about the baptisms and ministries of each, Jesus withdrew from Judea and headed back to Galilee.

Jesus' journey northward afforded another marvelous revelation into his life and ministry. The conversation with the woman by the well in Samaria by both action and word conveys many truths. This amazing encounter reveals insight into the inclusive nature of Jesus' ministry, the characteristics of true worship, and the way in which the good news about Jesus is spread.

In a sense no miraculous "sign" takes place in this event. Yet in another way it does. The very fact that Jesus met with this woman is a sort of sign, an amazing occurrence that was totally unexpected and out of the ordinary. Sometimes we look for miracles that involve only change in the material world, such as healing of the body, but a change in life and relationship can also be on the level of the miraculous. Such is the case in this event.

Nicodemus and the woman by the well were worlds apart in almost every way, and yet Jesus related to them in a similar way. The conversation between Jesus and each of them follows the same basic pattern. Jesus made a statement that was in keeping with the circumstance. The statement was misunderstood. Jesus cast the idea in an even more emphatic way. Nevertheless it was still not correctly understood. Then Jesus confronted the person and called for response.

This pattern provides an excellent example of a teaching technique from the Master Teacher. The best teaching calls for response, decision, and even action.

## Interpreting the Scriptures

### The Woman in Samaria (4:4–8)

**4:4.** The "had to" in this verse may relate primarily to geography. The shortest distance between Judea and Galilee was through Samaria. The Holy Land is only about 120 miles long, but in Jesus' day it had three distinct regions: Galilee in the north, Judea in the south, and Samaria in the middle. The Jordan River ran through all three regions from the Sea of Galilee in the north to the Dead Sea in the south. One travel route went north from Judea, across the Jordan River east, up the river to the area of Galilee, and then back across the river west. A shorter route was directly north from Judea through Samaria to Galilee. Thus, geographical distance may have been the reason for Jesus going through Samaria.

Another more important reason for the "had to" may have been to help establish that God's love was for all and that the ministry of Jesus was inclusive. Many Jews avoided the route through Samaria. Great enmity existed between the Samaritans and the Jews. The dislike, even hatred, of one for the other began centuries before Jesus' time. About 722 BC, Assyria conquered the northern part of the Holy Land, carried most of the population away, and replaced them with people who were not Jewish. Those who were carried away merged with the people in the area where they were taken and their identity as Jews was lost. Many of the Jews who were left in the area of Samaria married the foreigners who were brought to the region. This practice was contrary to Jewish law. The descendants of these people who did not stand strong for their Jewish faith lived in Samaria in Jesus' day.

Later, about 587 BC, Babylon conquered the southern part of the Holy Land and carried the people captive to Babylon. These captives remained faithful to the Jewish laws and customs. When they were allowed to return to Jerusalem, they returned "pure" and with disdain for the Samaritans, who had not remained "pure." Meanwhile the Samaritans had developed their own holy place and temple at Mount Gerizim. This added to the quarrel between the Jews and the Samaritans. The Samaritans sometimes harassed Jews who passed through Samaria. Too, the Jewish leaders wrote and spoke harsh words about the Samaritans. Thus when Jesus indicated that he "had to" pass through Samaria he may have been making the point that God loves all people, Jews and Samaritans alike.

**4:5–6.** About mid-day Jesus and his disciples stopped to rest by a well that had been dug centuries earlier by Jacob. The Gospel of John emphasizes the divine nature of Jesus, but it also makes clear Jesus' human nature. Thus John records that Jesus was tired from walking many miles. The main mode of transportation was walking, especially by a group such as Jesus and his disciples.

**4:7–8.** The disciples left Jesus alone by the well as they went into the nearby town of Sychar to buy food. A Samaritan woman from the town approached the well to draw water. Since a water supply likely existed in Sychar, why did she come to the well outside of the town? Quite possibly because of her moral condition she was excluded from the more convenient water supply. Too, coming at mid-day was also unusual because people using the well would have avoided the noon heat. Likely she hoped to avoid contact with other people. The well was deep, and a bag or jar to hold water tied to a rope had to be let down into the well to get water. Apparently the disciples had taken their water bag with them into town. Jesus thus made a simple request, "Will you give me a drink?"

## The Promise of Living Water (4:9–15)

**4:9.** Immediately the age-old feud between Jew and Samaritan surfaced. The woman recognized Jesus as a Jew. She stated the current social condition: "Jews do not associate with Samaritans." However, by talking with the woman, Jesus was crossing more barriers than the ancient one between Jew and Samaritan. Rabbis were forbidden to talk with women in public; Jesus, a rabbi, engaged the woman in conversation. Throughout his ministry Jesus lifted up the status of women and did not put them down as was the custom of that day. Furthermore, the woman was living with a man in an immoral relationship. For a religious leader to engage such a person in conversation other than for rebuke and condemnation was unheard of, and yet Jesus did just that.

**4:10.** Rather than arguing with the woman about the relation of Jews and Samaritans, Jesus indicated that if she had asked him for a drink he would have complied. In other words, he not only would talk with a Samaritan woman, but also he would meet her need for water. However, Jesus told her that he would provide "living water." On the physical level, living water was running water as in a stream, fresh and flowing, in contrast with water from most wells. Fresh, running water was preferred to pooled water. The water from the well apparently was not from an underground stream but from water that percolated into the cavity of the well. Thus Jesus was offering, even in physical terms, something better than she could get from the well.

**4:11–12.** The woman did not understand the spiritual content of Jesus' words about "living water." She took the words in their literal, physical meaning and saw that he had nothing with which to draw water. Furthermore, she felt that he was perhaps belittling the well since it did not have running or "living" water. So she emphasized the great heritage of the well all the way back to when it was first dug by Jacob.

**4:13–14.** Jesus contrasted the water from the well with the living water that he promised. He said the living water would create a spring within the person so that he or she would not have to go out to a source of water ever again. Similar to the concept of new birth, the picture is of a new kind of person with a spiritual resource within that constantly would cleanse, satisfy, and provide eternal life. This picture of life in Christ differs from that of the person who feels the need for a religious "fix" of some sort periodically. Jesus satisfies completely and eternally.

**4:15.** The woman either still did not understand or did not want to understand. She continued to speak in literal, physical terms.

## The Response of Faith (4:16–30, 39–42)

**4:16–18.** Jesus knew that the woman did not have a husband. She was living with a man who was not her husband. His words were intended to cut off the banter and get the woman to acknowledge her condition and need for the living water that he promised. We do not know what had happened to all of her five husbands. Death? Divorce? Abandonment? Jesus evidently mentioned this fact only to let the woman know that he knew all about her.

**4:19.** The woman's declaration indicated that she did not recognize Jesus for who he really was. She only knew that he could see her as she was, both past and present.

**4:20.** Why did the woman immediately launch an inquiry as to the proper place of worship? Quite likely it was because Jesus' statement about her condition had brought her face to face with her moral and spiritual need. She wanted to meet that need by worshipping in the correct way and place. Samaritans believed that Mount Gerizim was the true holy place; the Jews believed it to be Mount Zion.

**4:21–24.** Jesus' reply indicated that the place of worship really was not important and that the time was coming when people would realize that true worship did not depend on a place or ritual. Since God is spirit, true worship ought to be spiritual, not physical in a temple with the sacrifice of animals.

Jesus gives a special place to the Jews because God chose them as a means of revealing himself. God did not choose the Jews for special favor but for special service.

**4:25–26.** The Samaritan woman must have sensed that Jesus was more than a prophet. She spoke of the coming of the Messiah. Jesus confirmed that what she thought might be true was indeed true. Here is a clear statement from Jesus that he was indeed the Messiah. Jesus spent a great deal of his ministry clarifying the actual role of the Messiah.

**4:27.** The disciples returned from their food-buying trip to Sychar and found Jesus and the woman talking. They no doubt were amazed, probably even dismayed, to find Jesus talking with her. Yet they said nothing. By this time they had come to expect the unexpected from Jesus.

**4:28–30.** The woman was so excited about Jesus that she left her water jar when she ran to Sychar to tell the people about him. Obviously by leaving it she indicated that she planned to return. Her excitement was contagious. The townspeople came to see for themselves this person whom she thought might be the Messiah.

**4:39–41.** At first many of the Samaritans believed Jesus was the Messiah because of what he had told the woman. After two days of teaching they believed in him because of what he told them.

**4:42.** The Samaritans' faith became personal and individual, not second hand. The woman had asked a question (4:28), "Could this be the Christ?" After personal relation with Jesus, the people in Sychar declared he was more than the Jewish Messiah, he was "the Savior of the world." This title is in keeping with other accounts in John's Gospel (see 3:16; 12:19–21, 32).

## Focusing on the Meaning

Many barriers separate people from God and from one another. The event in this lesson shows Jesus crossing barrier after barrier to take the good news of God to people. The account also shows examples of people crossing barriers to come to a knowledge of and commitment to God in Christ.

How many barriers do you see in the story that Jesus had to cross in order to invite people into an intimate relationship with God and with one another? He crossed the barrier of geography, walking a great distance to Jacob's well and the area around Sychar. He crossed the barrier of prejudice, the prejudice of both Jews and Samaritans. He crossed the barrier of race and culture, for the Jews considered the Samaritans to be racially and culturally inferior. He crossed the barrier of gender, for he as a male Jew was not supposed to talk with a woman. He crossed the moral barrier, for he as the sinless Son of God visited with a woman whose lifestyle was immoral. He crossed the barrier of social custom, for he and his disciples as Jews were not supposed to fellowship with Samaritans, much less abide in one of their towns for days.

How many barriers do you see in the story that the Samaritans had to cross in order to come into a right relation with God? The woman crossed a language barrier, overcoming a literal understanding of words to comprehend the spiritual truth communicated by them. She crossed the barrier of traditional but wrong worship, beginning to gain the realization that a right relationship with God did not depend on ritual or place but on spirit and truth. The Samaritans crossed the barrier of a limited view of God's ability, coming to see that Jesus was not merely a prophet or even the Messiah but the Savior of the world.

Today we face many barriers in sharing the gospel. How many can you list? Each of them with God's help can be overcome. Today people also confront many barriers to a right relationship with God. How many can you name? With God's help we can aid them in overcoming these barriers.

# TEACHING PLANS

## Teaching Plan—Varied Learning Activities

### Connect with Life

1. Clip current events from recent newspapers related to human barriers people face (for example, discrimination, poverty, or illness). Before class distribute three or four clippings to members and ask them to prepare to summarize the event in their article. Call on members to share their summaries as the class period begins. Make the transition into the Bible study by reminding members that the study today indicates that Jesus crosses human barriers to invite all people into intimate relationship with God and with one another.

### Guide the Study

2. Read John 4:4–6 aloud. Explain why the Jewish people did not associate with Samaritans. Use the information in the short articles in the *Study Guide* on Samaria and Mount Gerizim and also the information in "Bible Comments" in this *Teaching Guide*.

3. Tell the class that no one is sure that John was married and obviously there was no such thing as a telephone in his day, but for the fun of it let us play like he was married and had a phone. Ask a previously enlisted member to read the cell phone conversation between John and his wife.

## A First-Century Cell Phone Conversation

Hello, dear! How are things? (pause)

I'm glad you're doing fine. I miss you too. (pause)

Well, I'm not sure when we'll be home. We're delayed in Sychar. (pause)

Sychar. That's in Samaria. (pause)

Jesus said he needed to go through here. (pause)

I don't know why. He just said he needed to, that's all. (pause)

They're not as bad as you've heard. Most of the people are real nice. (pause)

Well, we left Jesus at Jacob's well. (pause)

Yeah, Jacob came through here a long time ago. Anyway, we went to get some food in the city, and Jesus started talking to this woman who came to get some water. (pause)

Yes, to a woman. Jesus doesn't seem to care who he talks to. (pause)

No, dear, I don't talk to strange women. Uh! I mean I don't talk to any woman except you. (pause)

Yes, dear, you can trust me. Anyway, this woman accepted Jesus as the Messiah after he told her everything she had done. (pause)

Well, he told her she'd had five husbands and was living with a man who was not her husband. (pause)

I guess you could say that, but she's different now. (pause)

No, dear, I said you could trust me. She told the people of Sychar about Jesus and we're going to stay here a few days to talk to the people. I'll be home as soon as possible. (pause)

Yes, dear. You ought to know by now that I love you. How many times do I have to tell you? (pause)

I miss you, too. I'd better go now. These roaming charges are adding up. (pause)

I love you, too. Oh, I almost forgot the main reason I called. Tell Dad I'm sorry I'm missing out on going fishing with him. Bye.

4. Divide the marker board in half. On the top left side of the board write, *She Said.* On the top right side write, *He Said.* Under the *She Said* heading, write these verse numbers: 9, 11–12, 15, 17, 19–20, 25. Under the *He Said* heading, write these verse numbers: 7, 10,

13–14, 16, 17–18, 21–24, 26. Depending on the size of the class, make assignments to individuals or pairs using the verses listed under the headings. Ask members to find a key word, phrase, or summary statement in each of the assigned verses. After a period of study ask members to report as someone who prints well writes the responses on the board. After the reports lead the class to analyze the progression of the conversation, showing how Jesus responded to what the woman said.

5. Enlist a volunteer to read John 4:27–30 aloud. Refer to paragraph four under "Sharing the Gift" in the *Study Guide* (begins with "How did Jesus treat her?") and read the paragraph to the class. Ask members to respond to the thoughts given. Ask class members to discuss verse 29 in the light of more usual professions of faith (see paragraph five under "Sharing the Gift" in the *Study Guide*; begins with "After the woman had told . . . .).

6. Invite a volunteer to read John 4:39–42 aloud. Explore the two kinds of witnessing presented in this passage: personal testimony and preaching or teaching. Refer as needed to the ideas under "Knowing the Best Gift" in the *Study Guide.*

## Encourage Application

7. Erase the marker board and write these words at the top: *People I Meet in Places I Need to Go.* Ask everyone to think of places they go regularly and the names of people they meet in those places who need to make a commitment to Jesus Christ. Ask class members to call out the first names of these people. List the names on the board. Evaluate the list to determine those who are different socially, racially, economically, religiously, or in other ways. Explore the question: *What are some ways we can cross human barriers and help people come to know Jesus as Savior?* Close with prayer that class members will share their testimony and knowledge with people they know in places they need to go.

## Teaching Plan—Lecture and Questions

### Connect with Life

1. Display this lesson outline from the *Study Guide* on a marker board as follows:

> **If You Knew the Gift of God**
>
> 1. Receiving the Gift (John 4:4–26)
> 2. Sharing the Gift (John 4:27–30)
> 3. Knowing the Best Gift (John 4:39–42)

Lecture briefly on the Jewish-Samaritan relationship problems using the short article in the *Study Guide* titled "Samaria." Ask class members to suggest who some "Samaritans" are in today's society. Make the transition into the Bible study by reminding members that Jesus needed to go through Samaria and crossed human barriers to share his message.

### Guide Bible Study

2. Read "A First-Century Cell Phone Conversation" as a fun activity to introduce John 4:4–6. Read the verses aloud, and explain the setting briefly using information on the verses in "Bible Comments" in this *Teaching Guide*.

3. Invite a volunteer to read John 4:7–15 aloud. Lecture briefly on reasons most Jewish men would not have asked a Samaritan woman for a drink. Contrast what the woman thought about water to Jesus' idea of living water. Allow members to suggest ways to start conversations with people they do not know.

4. Read John 4:16–18 aloud. Ask, *Why do you think Jesus confronted the woman about her lifestyle by asking her about her husband? Why do you think the woman stayed around to continue the conversation?*

5. Enlist a volunteer to read John 4:19–26 aloud. Lecture briefly on the religious differences between Samaritans and Jews, using the short article in the *Study Guide* titled "Mount Gerizim" plus information

on these verses in this *Teaching Guide*. Include what Jesus taught her about true worship.

6. Read John 4:27–30 aloud. Ask, *Why do you think the woman went into town to tell the people about Jesus? Why do you think she left her water pot?*

7. Read John 4:39–42 aloud. Point out the two kinds of witnessing referenced in this passage: personal testimony and preaching or teaching. Suggest that people need to hear both kinds and that some people are better equipped to share a testimony and other people to teach or preach. Many people can do both.

## Encourage Application

8. Ask members to turn to the questions in the *Study Guide* and suggest answers.

9. On the marker board, write *Ways I Can Cross Human Barriers.* Invite members to suggest ideas they could use to cross barriers that usually hinder Christians from witnessing to people who are different.

## Focal Text

John 5:1–24, 31–40

## Background

John 4:43—5:47

## Main Idea

Jesus as God's Son has the authority to offer life in its fullness.

## Question to Explore

Why do you believe in Jesus?

## Teaching Aim

To lead the class to testify of why they believe in Jesus

## U N I T   O N E

**The Word and His Works**

# Lesson Five

# The Case for Jesus

## BIBLE COMMENTS

### Understanding the Context

After staying in Sychar two days sharing with the Samaritans, Jesus and the disciples resumed their journey north to Galilee. Arriving there they found the people celebrating what Jesus had done in Jerusalem. They were proud of their local hero. The residents of Judea in general and Jerusalem in particular often regarded people from Galilee as less than their equals. Therefore the Galileans were especially proud of Jesus.

Jesus returned to Cana, where he had turned water to wine, his first miracle recorded in John's Gospel. While there a government official came to him pleading for him to go to Capernaum and heal his sick son. Jesus told the man to return home and that his son would be well. Indeed the boy's fever left him at the very time Jesus promised the healing. This is the first healing by Jesus recorded in the Gospel of John. The people of Galilee rejoiced in the miracle.

Back in Jerusalem for a feast, Jesus performed another healing miracle. This time the response was not positive and led to a confrontation with Jewish religious leaders. The confrontation provided the setting for the first major discourse by Jesus recorded in the Gospel of John. Jesus took the opportunity to state the case for his being the Messiah, the Son of God.

To be understood fully the discourse by Jesus needs to be considered in light of the religious thought of the Jews at that time. Of course, even without knowledge of this Jewish religious thought, the words of Jesus are astounding. But given the context in which they were first delivered, they reveal not only who Jesus was but also his unconquerable courage.

Jesus' actions and words set him on a collision course with the Jewish religious leaders. After this speech had been delivered, there was no turning back for Jesus. The controversy would intensify until in the white heat of conflict the Jewish religious leaders would seek to eliminate Jesus by crucifixion. They failed, of course. Crucifixion was followed by Jesus' resurrection, ascension, and glorification.

Yet before the triumph of Jesus as King of Kings and Lord of Lords, months of miracles and teaching, acclaim and rejection, conflict and crisis, and finally pain and death would occur.


## Interpreting the Scriptures


### Jesus Heals an Invalid Man (5:1–15)

**5:1.** Jesus followed the basic requirements of the Jewish faith, such as those that called for Jewish males to participate in certain festivals at Jerusalem. He seemed to relish these times to identify with the feasts that celebrated the mighty acts of God in the history of the Hebrew people. After all, they commemorated his heavenly Father's actions in bringing redemption to lost humankind.

**5:2–5.** The pool's name, Bethesda, means "House of Mercy." However, in some manuscripts it is called Bethzatha, which means "House of Olives," and a section of Jerusalem was called Bethzatha. The pool was real, and the story is real. This is no parable or allegory.

Disabled people gathered around the pool because of a belief that when the water stirred, people entering it were healed. One of these people at the pool had been an invalid for thirty-eight years.

**5:6.** When Jesus saw the invalid man, Jesus asked him whether he wanted to get well. This may seem a strange question to ask a disabled person, but some people in that condition might not really want to get well. They have become accustomed to others taking care of them and do not want to assume the responsibilities of daily life. After all, after thirty-eight years the man likely had no marketable skills.

**5:7.** However, the man did want to be cured. His explanation for remaining an invalid was that when the water was stirred there was no one to take him into the pool for healing. While he struggled to drag himself into the pool, others entered first and were healed. Apparently the belief was that the first ones into the pool received the healing.

**5:8.** Jesus did not discuss with the man whether the pool had curative powers. Neither did he offer to place him in the pool. Instead he commanded him to get up, pick up the mat on which he had rested, and walk. One wonders what all of the other infirm people around the pool thought. Was there a clamor for Jesus to heal them also? Evidently there was not. Others may not even have been aware Jesus had been the agent of healing. Perhaps in the noise generated by all of the people around the pool, the voice of Jesus had been heard only by the man who was healed. Throughout Jesus' ministry one of the mysteries is why some were healed and others were not.

**5:9–13.** Immediately the man was cured. No slow process of healing and rehabilitation occurred as would be expected of healing by modern medicine. He did as Jesus told him to do and picked up his mat and walked. He walked right into trouble! The man was cured on the Sabbath. According to the interpretation of the Jewish law by the scribes and Pharisees, it was wrong to carry objects such as the mat on the Sabbath. Therefore the Jews confronted him. The former invalid gave as his reason for carrying the mat that the man who had cured him had told him to do so. The Jews then shifted at least part of the blame to the one who had healed him and demanded to know who it was. The man did not know Jesus and therefore could not identify him.

**5:14.** Later Jesus saw the man in the temple. His warning to him is difficult to interpret. What did Jesus mean by, "Stop sinning or something worse may happen to you"? A traditional belief in Jesus' time was that suffering was the direct result of a person's sin. A common reaction to someone's illness was to ask, *What sin did you commit that resulted in your being sick?* If the man believed that sickness was the result of sin and that he had in Jesus a cure for sickness, he may have felt that this freed him to sin. He thus did not have to worry about the consequences. Such a view would be similar to that of someone claiming to be a Christian and saying that since God forgives sin he or she will go on sinning. Evidently this latter viewpoint existed among church members in New Testament times (Romans 6:1–18; Galatians 5:13).

**5:15.** Why did the man tell the Jews that it was Jesus who had made him well? After all, he had previously said that he did not know who it was who had cured him. He may have done this because he was frightened of the consequences of breaking the regulations regarding the Sabbath. One of these rules from Jewish tradition stated that anyone carrying anything intentionally from a public place to a private house on the Sabbath was liable to punishment by death by stoning. To avoid such punishment he may have identified Jesus to shift the blame.

## Jesus Explains His Power (5:16–24)

**5:16.** The Jews indeed turned their attention to Jesus. He was the primary guilty party in their eyes.

**5:17–18.** Jesus' defense of his actions both startled and angered the Jews. He indicated that God was always at work, even on the Sabbath. In what way? Healing, judging, sustaining creation—God is at work in immeasurable ways all of the time. This statement might have irritated the Jews, but what really angered them was Jesus' claim to be working in the same way God was working and calling God his Father.

**5:19.** In response to the desire of the Jews to kill him, Jesus launched a lengthy discourse that served not to pacify the Jews but rather to intensify their hatred of him. The speech by Jesus confirmed in their minds that he was a blasphemer who claimed to be the Messiah and to be equal with God. Jesus clearly stated that the Father and the Son are as one in what they do.

**5:20.** The relation of Father and Son, Jesus declared, was one of love. Jesus said that because of the Father's love for the Son, the Son would do greater things than the Jews had observed in the healing of the invalid man. They had not seen anything yet!

**5:21.** The Father is the source of life and so is the Son. The life and death mentioned in this verse may refer to spiritual life and death, to physical life and death, or to both. Indeed, God the Father and Son give eternal life to those who are spiritually dead as well raise to life those who are physically dead.

**5:22.** The Father has given to the Son all judgment. Jesus elaborated on this in other places, such as his account of judgment recorded in Matthew 25:31–46.

**5:23.** The power of life and death and the right of judgment are given the Son that he may be honored as the Father is honored. If a person does not honor Jesus, the Son, that person does not honor God, the Father.

**5:24.** What Jesus shared with the people in Jerusalem on that Sabbath day centuries ago has meaning for people today. His words were not meant to be taken as theological debate but rather as a call to belief. The Jews who heard him were faced with decision. So are people today. Jesus is either the Son of God, the Messiah, the Savior of the world, or he is a maniacal blasphemer. No middle ground exists.

## Jesus Describes the Testimony About Himself (5:31–40)

**5:31–32.** Jesus' listeners wanted some evidence that what he said was true. According to Jewish law, two witnesses were necessary to confirm the validity of an alleged act or fact (Deuteronomy 17:6). Jesus acknowledged that his testimony alone would not be adequate. Therefore he offered the testimony of two others: John the Baptist and God, or more precisely the Scriptures given by God.

**5:33–35.** John the Baptist had testified clearly about the true nature of Jesus (1:19–34; 3:22–35). Jesus declared that he did not really need human testimony, but he referred to John because many of the Jews followed John and might accept his testimony. Jesus wanted to do everything possible to help the people believe in him. His desire was not to obscure the truth about himself. He wanted people to avoid the condemnation that would come to those who heard him speak and did not believe in him as the Son of God.

**5:36–38.** In addition to the human testimony of John the Baptist, Jesus called on the divine testimony of God the Father. The works that Jesus was doing, he pointed out, were the works of God. The very works should indicate that the Father and the Son are one. Yet because people refused to believe, God's word did not dwell in them.

**5:39–40.** Jesus declared that the Jews should know him because they diligently studied the Scriptures and the Scriptures testify of him. Yet they had come to worship the words of the Scriptures rather than the Word to whom the Scriptures testify. The Jews thought that they could find life in the words of Scripture, but of course they could not. Neither can we. Eternal life comes from Jesus, the Son of God, about whom the Scriptures testify.

## Focusing on the Meaning

In some ways the Jewish observers of Jesus' actions and listeners to his words were better equipped to understand the meaning of the actions and words than we are today. They were thoroughly versed in the teachings and traditions regarding the expected Messiah. They therefore recognized Jesus' actions as being in keeping with those of the promised deliverer of Israel who would usher in a new age (see Isaiah 35:6; Jeremiah 31:8–9). The words that Jesus used to describe himself were clearly claims of being the Messiah, including the titles "Son of Man" and "Son of God."

The Jews of Jesus' day also had a handicap in accepting him as the Messiah. They expected the Messiah to be a mighty deliverer, likely a military leader. Jesus simply did not fit the picture they had of the expected Messiah. He was a wandering teacher with a handful of disciples. How could he possibly deliver Israel from her enemies and usher in a new age of glory? To help overcome this misunderstanding Jesus spent a great deal of his teaching time prior to his crucifixion sharing the true picture of the Messiah as the Suffering Servant who would die for the sins of the people.

For Christians today the primary benefit of Jesus' actions and teachings is to provide testimony that he was indeed the Son of God, the Savior of the world. In bearing witness today, we can still utilize the actions and teachings of Jesus to demonstrate that he was and is the true Messiah of God. Reason and factual evidence are useful in helping people take the necessary leap of faith in Jesus as Lord and Savior.

The relation of the Father and the Son in the Trinity is a mystery, one beyond our human ability to fully comprehend or understand. Yet we can accept the words of Jesus that he and the Father are as one because of his works and character. Jesus' claims ring true. His testimony is solid. Therefore we urge people to believe in Jesus as God's Son our Savior, for we know that to reject the Son is to reject the Father. Life, abundant and eternal, comes to those who embrace the Son and therefore the Father.

# TEACHING PLANS

## Teaching Plan—Varied Learning Activities

### Connect with Life

1. Ask class members to suggest what motivated them to purchase certain kinds of automobiles (or some other item that is more appropriate to the class). List responses on the marker board. Make the transition into the Bible study by indicating that this lesson will help people identify reasons for believing in Jesus.

2. In advance, write the following on a poster:
   • Turning Water into Wine (John 2:1–11)
   • Healing the Royal Official's Son (John 4:46–54)
   • Healing the Man at the Pool of Bethesda (John 5:1–9)

   Refer to the poster and remind the class that the miracles listed are the first three miracles given as special signs in the Gospel of John and that the purpose of the study of John is to help people "believe that Jesus is the Messiah, the Son of God, and that by believing you may have life in his name" (John 20:31). Briefly summarize John 4:46–54, indicating that this event is the first healing reported in the Gospel of John.

### Guide Bible Study

3. In advance make a copy of the monologue "Healed!" and assign it to a good reader. Call on the reader to present the monologue now.

## Healed!

You can't imagine how I felt when this man came up to me and asked whether I wanted to be healed. I had been an invalid for thirty-eight years and had been trying to get in the pool of Bethesda when the water stirred. People told me the stirring waters might heal me. Friends carried me there day after day, but no one could stay around to put me in the pool at the right time.

Why would the man ask whether I wanted to be healed? Why else would I be there?

I figured he might volunteer to stay there long enough to put me in the pool, but he just told me to stand up, take my mat, and walk. Although I hadn't walked in a long time, I felt strength come into my legs as soon as he told me to get up. I did what he told me to do and was healed. What a miracle!

Some of the Jewish leaders were upset because I was carrying my mat on the Sabbath. Now let me ask you a question. Would you worry about disobeying the Sabbath law if you had just been healed after thirty-eight years? I told the leaders that a man healed me and told me to carry my mat. They wanted to know who told me to do that. I didn't know. I found out it was Jesus when I met him later at the temple. Jesus told me to stop sinning or something worse might happen to me. I don't know why Jesus chose to heal me out of all those people at the pool, but I'm glad he did.

Ask members to respond to the following questions:
- What are some possible reasons Jesus asked the man whether he wanted to be healed?
- Is there anything in the story indicating that the man had faith?
- Why did Jesus heal this man and not everyone else?

4. Divide the class into three listening teams. The team members should be near one another, but they do not need to move together. Assign teams to listen for the following:
   - *Team 1.* Listen for what Jesus asked the man who was healed to do.
   - *Team 2.* Listen for the concerns the religious leaders expressed.
   - *Team 3.* Listen for the defense Jesus gave for his actions.

Ask a volunteer to read 5:9b–24 aloud. After the reading ask members of the listening teams to talk to someone else on the team about the answers to their assignment. Call on volunteers to share with the class after a few moments of conversation. Clarify as needed from comments on these verses in this *Teaching Guide* and in the *Study Guide.* After the sharing ask everyone to look at verse 24 to determine what Jesus promises each person who believes.

5. Read 5:31–40 aloud. On the marker board, write *The Testimony of John the Baptist* on the left side and *The Testimony of the Old Testament* on the right side. Ask members to recall some things John did or said to testify about Jesus and list ideas under the heading. Repeat the process by asking members to recall some things the Old Testament says about the Messiah. Share insights as needed on these topics from comments on these verses in this *Teaching Guide.*

## Encourage Application

6. Prepare copies of the handout "Reasons I Believe in Jesus" and distribute to the class. As time allows, ask members to select the top three reasons they believe in Jesus and to share why they chose those reasons.

---

### Reasons I Believe In Jesus

\_\_\_\_ (1) Jesus has the power to change the lives of people.

\_\_\_\_ (2) Jesus testified that he is God's Son.

\_\_\_\_ (3) Jesus did God's work while he was here physically.

\_\_\_\_ (4) John the Baptist testified that Jesus is the Lamb of God.

\_\_\_\_ (5) Jesus fulfilled Old Testament prophecy.

\_\_\_\_ (6) Jesus changed my life.

\_\_\_\_ (7) Other _____

---

## Teaching Plan—Lecture and Questions

### Connect with Life

1. On the marker board, write *Things I Believe In.* Start the list with items like the law of gravity, the cycle of the seasons, the benefits of exercise, etc. Allow the class to suggest other items for the list. After several ideas have been shared, ask:

---

- Why do people believe in these items?
- How much of their belief relates to reason or experience and how much to faith?

Make the transition into the Bible study by saying that this lesson will suggest reasons for believing in Jesus.

2. Lecture briefly on the signs given in the Gospel of John. Point out that turning the water into wine (John 2:1–11), healing the royal official's son (4:46–54), and healing the man at the pool of Bethesda (5:1–9) are the first three signs. Point out that these signs in John's Gospel help people "believe that Jesus is the Messiah, the Son of God, and that by believing you may have life in his name" (John 20:31).

## Guide Bible Study

3. Prepare the handout, "Notes on John 5:1–24, 31–40." Present a lecture based on the Bible passage and the suggested outline. Use

---

### Notes on John 5:1–24, 31–40

1. A Strange Healing (John 5:1–9a)
   a. Reasons Jesus asked the man whether he wanted to be healed

   b. Ideas related to the power of Jesus to heal instead of the faith of the man

2. A Strange Conflict (John 5:9b–24)
   a. The testimony of the man who was healed

   b. The problems of the Jewish leaders

   c. The defense of Jesus

3. A Strong Witness (John 5:31–40)
   a. The testimony of John the Baptist

   b. The testimony of the Old Testament

---

information on these passages in the *Study Guide* and in this *Teaching Guide*. Be sure to provide information for each point listed, and encourage the class to take notes. After the lecture, review the notes briefly.

## Encourage Application

4. Relate a life situation like the following:

   Craig and Heather are neighbors to a Christian couple named Michael and Susan. Michael and Susan have taken seriously their responsibility to relate to non-believers, and they have included Craig and Heather in their circle of friends. The two couples often get together for social events along with other couples in the community. One night Craig and Heather came over to Michael and Susan's patio. The conversation eventually turned to reasons Michael and Susan believe in Jesus. Suppose Michael and Susan had studied this lesson on the Sunday before. What reasons could they give Craig and Heather based on John 5? What other reasons could they give?

   Ask the class to suggest the reasons Michael and Susan might have given. Write them on the marker board.

5. Refer to question 4 in the *Study Guide*. Ask members to use the back side of the handout to write reasons they believe Jesus is the Son of God. After a few minutes, invite comments.

## Focal Text

John 6:41–58, 66–69

## Background

John 6—8

## Main Idea

Jesus calls us so to commit ourselves to him that we base every aspect of our lives on him.

## Question to Explore

Do you believe in Jesus because of what he does for you or because of who he is?

## Teaching Aim

To lead the class to state the significance for their lives of Jesus as the bread of life and evaluate the extent of their commitment to him

## UNIT TWO

**The Growing Conflict**

## Lesson Six

# To Whom Shall We Go?

## BIBLE COMMENTS

### Understanding the Context

Back in Galilee Jesus continued to perform many wonderful signs, or miracles. Chapter six of the Gospel of John records two of the most astounding—(1) Jesus feeding a multitude of people with only five loaves of barley bread and two small fish plus (2) Jesus walking on water in the midst of a storm on the Sea of Galilee.

The feeding of the multitude caused the crowd to want to make Jesus their king (6:15) because he could miraculously provide food (6:26) just as God provided manna for the Hebrews in their wilderness wanderings (Exodus 16). Jesus refused.

The miracle also led to Jesus teaching about his being the bread of life that had come down from heaven. This teaching offended Jewish leaders and led to further confrontation. Later in Jerusalem the conflict intensified as Jesus elaborated on who he was and what he had come to do. Those who listened to Jesus and to the charges against him by Jewish leaders were divided in their opinions about him. Some thought him to be a good man. Others considered him demon-possessed. Many apparently accepted the charge against him of making false claims about being the Messiah because he supposedly came from Galilee and the prophecies indicated that the Messiah was to come from Judea. In spite of the rising opposition to Jesus the authorities were not able to bring about his arrest. Too many people considered Jesus to be a good man for that to happen at this time.

During this period in Jesus' ministry the fair-weather disciples who followed him only because of his miracles of healing and feeding began to drop by the wayside. Some apparently found his teachings too difficult either to comprehend or to follow. Others likely began to fear association with him because of the increasing enmity toward Jesus by the religious establishment. To be a disciple of Jesus was becoming risky. Some were not willing to take the risk.

Other disciples continued to follow Jesus, seeking to better understand who he really was and what the terms of discipleship really were. These disciples were learning to believe in Jesus not only for what he did in miraculous signs but also, even primarily, for who he was—the bread of life, the light of the world, the Son of God, the Son of Man, the Christ!

## Interpreting the Scriptures

### Jesus Teaches that He Is the Bread of Life (6:41–52)

**6:41.** Jesus used the discussion with the Jewish leaders to correct the misunderstanding that they had about him and his message. He taught to clarify as he had with Nicodemus (3:1–16) and the Samaritan woman (4:4–42).

People grumbled a lot about what Jesus said. His words were disturbing to the Jews for many reasons, but primarily because they seemed blasphemous. Jesus' words exalted him to equality with God. His words clearly set forth his claim to be the expected Messiah because the Jews knew well the titles and actions ascribed to the Messiah in the literature and traditions about him. Yet Jesus did not fit their preconceived notions of the Messiah. Therefore, his claiming to be the Messiah angered them. This encounter with the Jewish leaders shows the growing resistance and hostility to Jesus (see also 7:25, 32–36, 40–52; 8:37–59).

**6:42.** One of the reasons the Jews rejected the claims of Jesus was Jesus' humble origin and social status. This particular passage chronicles events in Galilee, the region in which Jesus grew up and spent his early adult years. The people knew Joseph, his earthly father, and Mary, his mother. Joseph had been a carpenter (Matthew 13:55). Apparently Jesus had followed Joseph's trade (Mark 6:3). "Familiarity breeds contempt" is a common saying and may have applied to the situation with Jesus and his fellow Galileans. Joseph and perhaps Jesus himself had likely built tables and chairs for them and perhaps helped construct their houses. How could a common worker be someone who had come down from heaven?

Furthermore, Jesus' claim to be the Messiah struck them as false. They expected the Messiah to be a mighty figure who would throw off the heavy yoke of Roman rule and restore Israel to independent power. To them Jesus was a carpenter, not a mighty leader, teacher, or military genius.

**6:43.** Jesus was well aware of the grumbling going on among the Jews. He knew that they would find no answers to life's major questions talking to themselves. They needed to heed the voice of God, to listen to Jesus.

**6:44.** The word translated "draws" is the same word for drawing a sword from its scabbard or drawing a net filled with fish. In almost every case that the word is used it relates to a pull of something that has resistance. In other words, God draws people to himself, but often they resist. This verse does not deny that people have free will, that they are able to make choices. The biblical concept of soul competency makes clear that people do have choices and are responsible for the choices that they make. In a sense, however, the ability of a person to choose God depends on God's drawing that person to himself. Soul competency is not a human creation but a divine gift. Jesus indicates that God "draws" people to himself and those who respond will be raised "up at the last day." Here he was speaking of the resurrection of the dead. Some Jews believed in the resurrection of the dead; others did not. Jesus affirmed the possibility of resurrection.

**6:45.** Jesus' words indicate that all people have the potential of coming to God for eternal life. Those who understand God's word about Jesus will want to believe in Jesus. Those who refuse to understand will not believe.

**6:46.** The Scriptures state that no mortal has seen God. Jesus declared that he has seen the Father. The implication is clear: Jesus is related to God as no one else has been, is, or will be. He is God's Son.

UNIT TWO: The Growing Conflict

**6:47.** Those who are drawn to God and who open their hearts and minds to understanding, believe in Jesus. These have "everlasting life"—"eternal life" (NASB, NRSV). In the next verses Jesus indicates why this is true.

**6:48.** Those who believe in Jesus have everlasting life because he is the "bread of life." Bread was the basic food staple of the ancient world. Bread was the symbol of life.

**6:49.** Yet Jesus is no ordinary bread. He is even more wonderful than the type of bread supplied the children of Israel as they wandered in the wilderness—manna. The Hebrews ate the manna, a miraculous food supplied by God, but they all eventually died.

**6:50.** Jesus promised bread that when eaten would provide eternal life. Remember that he also promised an internal spring of living water that would be everlasting (4:14).

**6:51.** With this verse begins a passage that is somewhat difficult for modern readers to interpret and was difficult for Jesus' Jewish hearers to accept. He indicated that he was the living bread, that is, the bread that provides the ability to "live forever." By Jesus' statement that he would give this bread, his flesh, for the life of the world, he was speaking of his incarnation and crucifixion. What did he mean by eating the bread, that is, his flesh?

**6:52.** Jesus' statement troubled the Jews. They wondered how Jesus could give them his flesh to eat.

## Jesus Clarifies His Teaching (6:53–58)

**6:53–55.** Jesus answered the question posed by the Jews. His words have been interpreted in various ways. The branches of the Christian movement that believe in transubstantiation (that is, that at the Lord's Supper or the Mass the elements of bread and juice are transformed into the actual flesh and blood of Jesus) point to this passage as evidence of the validity of their view. Those of us who hold that the bread and juice are symbols of Jesus' body and blood, of course, reject that interpretation.

A symbolic interpretation seems best to fit the passage. Jesus did not indicate that people would need to eat his actual flesh and drink his literal blood in order to have eternal life. He did intend that we be so vitally related to him that we would almost become as one with him as we become almost one with bread and juice when we consume them.

**6:56–57.** Jesus delivered this teaching in the synagogue (6:59). Those who heard were Jews. However, the people in the synagogue were also familiar with pagan religions. The concepts of becoming united with a god and of figuratively eating the flesh of a god were not foreign to them, although of course they did not accept such beliefs.

The adherents of what are called the "mystery religions" of that day believed in a god who suffered, died, and came back to life. Initiates into the religion took part in an elaborate ceremony in which the story of the god was dramatized. They supposedly united with the god in an ecstatic experience. In pagan worship, animal sacrifice was common. In offering the sacrifice the priest usually placed only part of the carcass on the altar to be consumed; the rest was eaten by the priests and sometimes by the worshippers. It was believed that the god being worshipped entered the body of the animal sacrificed and therefore those who ate of the animal in a sense also ate of the god. Of course, such religions were false. Jesus was not affirming them in any way. However, as was his custom, he did use well-known experiences to communicate spiritual truth.

**6:58.** Even apart from the backdrop of these false religions, the words Jesus used conveyed the idea of life. Bread was food, and food was necessary to sustain life. Blood was essential for life in the body. The bread and blood that Jesus offered are eternal. Thus by believing in Jesus and becoming as one with him a person has eternal life. Nothing else can provide such life. Any other bread, even the manna from heaven, does not provide eternal life. Those who eat of such bread will eventually die.

### Jesus Calls For Decision (6:66–69)

**6:66.** Some of the people who had been following Jesus as a teacher found this teaching "hard" (6:60). For many it may have been hard to understand. For others it was hard to accept. Jesus clearly was calling for complete commitment to him, in a sense for union with him. As a result a number of the disciples "turned back and no longer followed him."

**6:67–68.** Jesus asked the twelve disciples, the inner group of his followers, whether they would leave also. Peter answered for the group that they would remain with Jesus because he had the words of eternal life.

The disciples of Jesus were called on to make radical choices. So are people today. Some then were not willing to make the radical commitment that Jesus' teachings demanded, just as some today are not.

**6:69.** Having witnessed first hand the miraculous signs of Jesus and heard his amazing words, Peter concluded that Jesus was "the Holy One of God." This is similar to Peter's confession, "You are the Christ, the Son of the living God" (Matthew 16:16). Apparently Peter was speaking for the other disciples as well, but Jesus knew already that one of them, Judas, would betray him (John 6:70). Peter and the others had much yet to learn about Jesus. Yet they understood enough at this point to give Jesus their allegiance.

The fact that the disciples had the ability to choose between following Jesus and rejecting him indicates what Baptists call "soul competency." Each person has the God-given ability—and responsibility—to choose to trust and obey Jesus. God in his sovereignty provides us freedom of choice.

## Focusing on the Meaning

This account describes a sort of watershed in the ministry of Jesus. Up to this point, opposition to him had been strong, but he also had a large following, especially in his home region of Galilee. In fact, even when the Jews in Jerusalem had plotted against him he was welcomed as a home-town hero in Galilee. Now that began to change. Many who had followed him drifted away.

Why? What brought about the change? Is there a truth for us in this situation?

To be sure, some likely turned away for fear of association with Jesus. His teachings had aroused the ire of powerful Jewish leaders. Continuing to follow Jesus put a person's business, social standing, and reputation at risk, perhaps even his or her life. And some may have followed in hopes of being cured of illness or getting a free meal. It was becoming clear, however, that not everyone would be healed and the free meals were few and far between. So they dropped out.

John's account, however, does not seem to focus on these as the primary reasons for a falling away of followers. Apparently a number of people began to realize that following Jesus involved more than hearing fascinating stories and witnessing marvelous signs. Jesus began to call for commitment, for total commitment to him. He indicated that apart from literally becoming one with him through believing in him there was no hope of eternal life. Many were unwilling to abandon self-interests for the Savior.

Isn't the same true today? Some people turn away from Jesus because of fear of what others would think of their becoming his followers. Some choose not to follow because they sought a circus atmosphere of signs and wonders and found instead in Christ a service lifestyle. However, don't most people fail to follow Jesus because of his demand to deny self, take up their cross, and follow him daily? (See Matt. 16:24–26.) The call of Jesus is not basically to religion, theological discussion, or ritual but to total, unreserved commitment to him as both Lord and Savior. Some are not willing to make such a leap of faith.

# TEACHING PLANS

## Teaching Plan—Varied Learning Activities

### Connect with Life

1. After welcoming the class and opening with prayer, lead the class in the following opening activity. Ask, *How many have played the game Trivial Pursuit™?* Call for a show of hands. Invite the class to begin the lesson by playing a game. Distribute paper and pencils, and instruct the class members to answer *True* or *False* to the following questions (allow them to work with a partner if they want to):
   (1) Bananas grow on banana trees. (False. There is no such thing as a banana tree. The plant is a large herb.)
   (2) The tomato is a vegetable. (False. It is a berry, a fruit.)
   (3) The sun came up this morning. (False. Of course, the earth revolves.)

   Review the answers with the group. Explain that one definition of "myths" is that they are unexamined, strongly-held beliefs that often do not allow us to see the truth. Note that the idea of a flat earth was such a belief until the end of the fifteenth century AD.

2. As the learners prepare to read the Bible passage, explain that today's lesson will illustrate how strongly held beliefs and assumptions can become an impediment to faith.

3. To provide a visual and symbolic focal point for the learners, unveil or place a loaf of bread on a small table at the center of the room or in a central location where everyone can see. You may choose to refer to the bread overtly, or you can let the symbol speak for itself throughout the lesson.

## Guide Bible Study

4. Distribute listening guides you've prepared ahead of time. Each listening guide should have one of the following words written on it: *Who? What? When? Where? How?* Each learner is to receive only one sheet and is instructed to answer the question on the listening guide as they listen to and follow the reading of the text. Enlist a volunteer to read John 6:41–58 aloud while the class members listen.

5. Underscore the context of the passage by referring to the feeding of the multitudes in 6:1–14. Help learners grasp the basic content of 6:41–58 by having them share quickly their responses from the listening guides. Prompt the learners by challenging them to clarify, amplify, and explain their responses. Add further explanation to help the learners understand the passage (refer to the *Study Guide* and the comments on these verses in this *Teaching Guide* for information). Highlight the following: (a) the theological meaning of the feeding of the multitudes; (b) the response of the crowd to the bread Jesus provided; (c) Jesus' refusal of kingship.

6. Encourage the learners to identify the "myths" held by the people and the Jewish leaders that did not allow them to see the truth of the work and person of Jesus (possible answers: expectation of a different kind of Messiah; belief that discipleship was unnecessary; belief that main goal of Messiah's coming was to provide for them physically rather than to call them to service and faithfulness). Continue to interpret the passage through dialogue by asking open-ended questions such as these: *Why do you think . . . ? What if . . . ? What question do you have . . . ?"*

7. Invite a volunteer to read 6:66–69 aloud as the rest listen for the major concern of the passage. Call for comments. Point out that Jesus' statements resulted in two extreme responses. Some disciples left him while others believed more deeply. Before moving on to the next step, invite members to ask questions they have about these verses. Pause and give members time to formulate and ask questions. Follow up on questions from the class members. Invite discussion of what the passage suggests for application to our lives.

## Encourage Application

8. Distribute the "Application Questions" you've prepared ahead of time. Have class members form groups of three to four (no more than four to a group). Instruct them to work through the questions, being sure to answer question four. Allow about ten-to-twelve minutes.

---

### Application Questions

*Instructions*: Choose a timekeeper/prompter for your group to help you stay on track and keep things moving. You do not have to answer every question, but be sure to answer question four.

(1)Does "following Jesus" mean the same today as it did to the disciples?

(2)With whom do you most identify in today's story: the people hungering for bread, the disciples, the religious leaders, Peter, or the people who wanted to make Jesus king? Share why you feel that way.

(3)In today's passage, Peter made his confession of faith in Jesus. When and where did you make your confession?

(4)Share two of your reasons for "following Jesus."

(5)In two sentences state why this passage is important for (a) the believer in Christ and (b) the unbeliever.

---

9. Allow as much time as possible for the groups to do their work. Alert the group two minutes before calling them together, reminding them that they must answer question four. Call time at least five minutes before you need to bring the class session to a close.

---

UNIT TWO: The Growing Conflict

10. Invite each group to share their responses to question four of the "Application Questions." Close the class session with a guided prayer in which you lead members to evaluate their personal commitment to Jesus as the Bread of Life. (Option: Participate in a communion fellowship by having class members pass the bread to each other, saying, "Jesus is the Bread of Life.")

## Teaching Plan—Lecture and Questions

### Connecting with Life

1. Welcome the class members and open the class session with prayer. Fashion your prayer so as to focus on Jesus as the Bread of Life.

2. Recall an episode in your life in which you either misunderstood someone or in which someone misunderstood you to disastrous or humorous result. Share that story with the class. After you have shared your experience, ask, *What experience have you had in which you were misunderstood?* Invite responses.

3. Help the learners know where they are going with today's lesson by stating that at the end of the class session they will be asked to (a) consider the significance of Jesus as the Bread of Life and (b) evaluate the extent of their commitment to him.

### Guide Bible Study

4. Explain that today's Scripture passage contains a story of a misunderstanding with tragic results. Point to an outline of today's lesson that you've written on the board or on a poster:

> ### To Whom Shall We Go?
> 1. Christ, the Bread of Life (John 6:41–51)
> 2. Appropriating Jesus As the Bread of Life (John 6:52–58)
> 3. Peter's Great Confession (John 6:66–69)
> 4. Application for Living

5. Summarize the feeding of the multitude in 6:1–14 as background for the conversation between the Jewish leaders and Jesus. Describe what feeding meant to the multitude in the context of the passage. Make reference to Exodus 16 and explore with the class reasons Jesus refused to be crowned king (6:15). Provide information from "Understanding the Context" in this *Teaching Guide.*

6. Enlist a volunteer to read 6:41–58 aloud. Instruct the rest of the class to listen specifically for these points: (a) Jesus' declaration about himself; (b) the misunderstanding; (c) the clarification. (You might choose to have three class members read the text in "parts": the narrator, Jesus, and the Jews—"they"—using the Scripture text printed in the *Study Guide.*)

7. Guide the class in exploring the text by engaging them in a dialogue about various verses in 6:41–58. Encourage the conversation by asking questions like these:
   • What did Jesus say? What did he mean by that?
   • In what way did the Jews misunderstand what Jesus said?
   • Why do you think they misunderstood Jesus?
   • Why do you think Jesus did not put it another way so as not to be misunderstood? In what way or why not?

8. Ask the class to help you paraphrase verses 52–58 in a way that can be understood by a contemporary hearer. On the board or flip chart, write and edit the paraphrase as the class attempts to arrive at an accurate interpretation. Or simply put the verses in your own words.

9. Encourage the class now to consider 6:66–69, especially how it applies to their lives. Invite someone to read the passage aloud.

10. Explain the passage, using information in the *Study Guide* and in this *Teaching Guide.* Be certain to explain Peter's use of the term, "the Holy One of God" (6:69). Point out that there were two responses to Jesus' self-identification: some left and some confessed their faith in Jesus. Point out that some believed in Jesus only because of what he did for them (provided bread) and some because of who he said he was (the Bread of Life).

## Encourage Application

11. Ask: *Do you believe in Jesus because of what he does for you or because of who he is?* Give the class members a few moments to think about the question, and then ask for responses. Accept responses without commentary or attempting to "correct" answers. Allow plenty of time for this response. Pause and wait expectantly until most of the class answers. Encourage the class now to consider the extent of their commitment to Jesus. Ask, *Are you truly following Jesus as Lord, or do you just want Jesus to give you various things?* Close the class session with a prayer of confession and thanks for Jesus as the Bread of Life.

## Focal Text

John 9:1–7; 9:39—10:19

## Background

John 9—10

## Main Idea

Jesus provides abundant life to all who will let him open their eyes.

## Question to Explore

We couldn't be blind, could we?

## Teaching Aim

To lead the class to identify ways in which they themselves could be spiritually blind

**UNIT TWO**

*The Growing Conflict*

# Lesson Seven

# The Good Shepherd and Human Blindness

## BIBLE COMMENTS

### Understanding the Context

Jesus continued to present his claims to be the Son of God in spite of growing opposition. He demonstrated his courage by teaching in the temple courts (John 8:2). This was the stronghold of those Jews most antagonistic to him. Here Jesus declared himself to be "the light of the world" (8:12). This phrase echoes the prologue of John's Gospel: "The light shines in the darkness, but the darkness has not understood it. . . . The true light that gives light to every man was coming into the world" (1:5, 9). Jesus' teaching that those who did not believe in him lived in darkness further infuriated the Jewish leaders.

In response to Jesus' claims to be the Son of God his enemies countered that he was a demon-possessed Samaritan. Few character assessments could have been worse in Jewish society. Samaritans were hated half-breeds according to the Judean Jews. Demon possession, thought to be common, was feared. Jesus countered that he was not demon possessed because "before Abraham was born, I am" (8:58). The Jews considered Abraham, the great patriarch, as the father of the nation. Jesus' declaring himself superior to Abraham and stating that he existed before Abraham was born brought on an attack by the Jews to kill Jesus. Jesus, though, escaped the stoning.

Why weren't the Jews able to capture Jesus or to kill him by stoning? Jesus often stated that "the hour" or "his time" had not yet come (see 2:4; 7:6; 8:20; 12:23, 27; 13:1; 17:1). This would have been the time in God's plan for his sacrificial death on the cross. Thus in a sense Jesus was protected by God's timetable. Also, Jesus' confrontation with the Jewish authorities took place under the watchful eye of Roman soldiers who were charged to keep the peace. The Jews realized that to stone Jesus would likely create a riot since he still had many followers. The Roman authorities would severely punish those who instigated the riot.

Thus the context for the present lesson presents Jesus calmly going about his ministry in the midst of threats to his life. Not only did he continue to perform miracles, but he also persisted in teachings that infuriated the Jews as he presented claims to be the divine Son of God.

## Interpreting the Scriptures

### Jesus Heals a Blind Man (9:1–7, 39–41)

**9:1–2.** Jesus performed miracles "as he went along" and encountered people in need, such as the blind man. This is the first miracle of healing by Jesus recorded in John's Gospel where a person had been afflicted from birth. Such a condition raised a theological issue with the Jews. They believed that suffering was a direct result of a person's sin. Therefore a congenital defect presented a problem: How could this person's blindness be the result of sin since he had been blind from birth? Some Jewish scholars solved the problem by declaring that even in the womb the fetus could sin. Others ascribed the sin to the parents since the Old Testament stated that the sins of the parents are visited upon the children (Exodus 20:5; but see also Ezekiel 18:4).

**9:3.** Jesus refused to assign blame to the man or to his parents. Instead he focused on the opportunity to minister to need. By his silence Jesus may have been indicating that suffering is not necessarily the direct result of a person's sin. Therefore an attempt to assign blame is wrong. Jesus did not teach that God made the man blind so that Jesus could perform a miracle. Instead, Jesus taught that the fact of the man's blindness provided opportunity for ministry that would display the power of God in Jesus' life.

**9:4.** The opportunity for witness and ministry does not last forever. A time comes when opportunity exists no longer. This is when "night" has come. Hard work is called for in ministry while there is opportunity; that is, while "it is day."

**9:5.** Jesus' statement reemphasizes the urgency of ministry. His light would not always be in the world.

**9:6–7.** In this instance the purpose of the miracle seems to have been the demonstration of the power of God in Jesus to heal, to do good, as a kind of rebuttal to the charges of the Jews against him.

**9:39.** Verses 8–38 show that the man's healing created quite a commotion, with conversations by the man's neighbors among themselves and with the man (9:8–12), by the Pharisees with the man's parents and with the man himself (9:13–34), and by the man with Jesus (9:35–38). The day on which the healing occurred was the Sabbath. Therefore the Pharisees quizzed the man to determine whether any Jewish laws regarding the Sabbath had been broken in his healing. When the man said that Jesus had made mud for his eyes, the Pharisees declared that the Sabbath had been broken because no work was to be done on the Sabbath and making this mud in their narrow legalistic view consisted of work (9:14–16). The Pharisees insisted that Jesus could not possibly be from God because he was breaking the laws regarding the Sabbath. When the man persisted in his belief that Jesus was doing good, the Pharisees "threw him out" (9:34). The meaning may be that he was put out of the synagogue, the Jewish place of worship (see 9:22). Jesus heard about this drastic action, sought the man, and witnessed to him. The man believed in Jesus and "worshiped him."

In response to the man's profession of faith Jesus indicated that he had come so that the blind could see. The man who had been blind had been made to see physically. He had also been brought to see spiritually that Jesus was indeed the Son of Man. However, those who thought they saw clearly the things of God were shown by Jesus' presence to be blind spiritually.

**9:40–41.** The Pharisees realized that Jesus was accusing them of blindness. Thus they confronted him with the question, "Are we blind too?"

UNIT TWO: The Growing Conflict

The "blindness" of which Jesus spoke was spiritual, not physical, of course. Jesus said that if the Pharisees had not known all of the prophecies and information about the coming Messiah, their failure to believe in him might be forgiven. However, since they should have known who he was, their "guilt remains."

## Jesus Teaches About the Good Shepherd (10:1–19)

**10:1–5.** Jesus continued his discussion with the Pharisees, stating that he is the Good Shepherd. The chapter divisions are not original with the Gospel of John, and the section on the Good Shepherd is related to the healing of the blind man. Once again Jesus' description of himself was similar to that used in the Old Testament to describe God (Psalm 23).

Raising sheep was common. Each flock of sheep had a shepherd. The shepherd was responsible for the sheep. The sheep were totally dependent on the shepherd. Since the sheep were used mainly for wool and not for meat, a shepherd might have the same sheep for years, often giving them names. A bond developed between the shepherd and the sheep so that the sheep trusted the shepherd, knew his voice, and responded to his call.

If a sheep pen were available, flocks of various shepherds would be herded into the pen at night for safety. A watchman would be posted to guard the gate to the pen. Only shepherds of the sheep that were inside the pen would be allowed in, and they would enter only by the gate. Therefore if anyone entered any other way, he would be a thief and a robber. The watchman would let the shepherds in, and the shepherds would separate the flocks by each shepherd calling out his own sheep. The sheep would know and trust his voice and follow him; they would never follow a stranger.

**10:6.** Jesus used the figure of speech of the shepherd and the sheep to refer to himself. The Pharisees, and perhaps the disciples as well, did not understand the meaning of his words. Likely he also had in mind the blind man when he spoke of the "sheep."

**10:7.** By referring to himself as "the gate," Jesus indicated that he was the way to safety. In some instances a place for the sheep to rest in safety at night did not have walls and a door as such. It had only a fence and an open area that served as a "gate" for the sheep to enter and depart. The shepherd would sleep at night at this open area. He would prevent wild animals and thieves from entering. Thus Jesus described himself as both the gate and the shepherd.

**10:8.** Perhaps Jesus in this verse was referring to the Pharisees, who stole from the people a true knowledge of God and robbed them of the abundant life that could be theirs in Christ. Or he may have been referring to false prophets who stirred the people to false hope and often led them to catastrophe. The sheep of Christ's fold, however, listen only to his voice.

**10:9–10.** By trusting in Jesus as the gate or way to salvation, people enter not only into safety but also to full and abundant life, finding "pasture."

**10:11–13.** Jesus foretold his death on the cross. Just as the good shepherd was willing to die for the welfare of his sheep, the Good Shepherd was willing to die for the salvation of the world. Faced with danger, the hireling shepherd would run, sacrificing the sheep to save his life. The owner shepherd on the other hand would sacrifice his safety for the security of his sheep. That is the kind of shepherd Jesus indicated that he was.

**10:14–15.** Jesus revealed that the relationship of the Good Shepherd and his sheep is like the relationship of Jesus and his Father. Those who trust and follow Jesus are as close to him as Jesus is to his Father.

**10:16.** Not only the Jews who trusted and followed Jesus were to be part of his flock but also any who heard his voice and trusted and followed. Jesus concentrated his ministry on the Jews, but he did not ignore others.

The concept of "one flock" is found in other places in the Bible (Ezekiel 34:23; 37:24). Jesus was not speaking of ecclesiastical organizations but of individual relationship with him. A flock does not exist because sheep that are all alike congregate. Rather, a flock is made up of sheep that relate to a particular shepherd and respond to his voice and leadership. Likewise the flock of Jesus is not composed of people who are all alike or belong to the same church organization but of people who relate to him in trust and followship.

**10:17–18.** The Father loves the Son because of his obedience, even to death. The Father's love for the Son is not conditional but unconditional. Yet in some way beyond our understanding the Father's love was intensified by Jesus' unconditional obedience, even to death on the cross.

Jesus indicated that he had a choice in the matter of his death. He would submit to death voluntarily. It was not forced on him. He had authority to accept or to reject the death. The Father told him that he had this authority. Jesus chose to accept the death. He also realized that he would take up his life again, a reference to his resurrection.

**10:19.** The teaching of Jesus about being the Good Shepherd followed the miracle of healing the man born blind. The teaching apparently was intended to explain why Jesus had the power to heal in such a miraculous way: Jesus was one with the Father and obedient to the Father.

The Jews were divided over the teaching and the miracle. The division among the Jews did not diminish as Jesus continued to teach in Jerusalem. They insisted that he tell them plainly whether he was the Christ. Jesus' teaching so infuriated some of the Jews that they took up stones to kill him, but he escaped once more unharmed.

## Focusing on the Meaning

The people of Jesus' day disagreed about who Jesus really was. Some did not believe the testimony about him. Others misinterpreted his actions. Many misunderstood his teachings for various reasons. Such is the case with people today. You likely know people who fit into each of these categories. By being "blind" to Jesus, people cut themselves off from his blessings. Some, however, believed that Jesus was the promised Messiah of the Jews and the Savior of the world.

The accounts of Jesus' actions and teachings recorded in John's Gospel make one thing very clear: a person cannot remain neutral about Jesus. Some try, of course. They say something like this: *He was a good man but not the Son of God. No decision about him is really necessary.* Of course, how could this be true? If he were a good man he would not lie about being the Son of God; yet over and over his actions and words conveyed his belief that he was indeed the Son of God.

Thus the choices about Jesus are really only two. These choices were reflected in the response of the Jews to Jesus: (1) he was a bad person, either a madman or a liar; or (2) he was the divine Son of God. The evidence points to the latter. Jesus' miraculous actions are not those of a madman or a bad person. He went about doing good. His miracles were not for his benefit but for the benefit of others.

Those who knew him best did not think of him as either a liar or insane. His disciples, those closest to him, after considering all the evidence first hand, declared him to be not a maniac but the Messiah. John the Baptist declared him to be the Lamb of God that takes away the sins of the world. Millions of people through the centuries have heard the good news about Jesus and believed; their lives have been forever changed.

Thus every one of us must make a decision about Jesus. Have you decided that he is the Son of God and trusted and followed him? Those of us who know Jesus as the Son of God have responsibility not only to share the good news about him but also to urge people to believe in him. Jesus died for us. Now we are to live for him.

# TEACHING PLANS

## Teaching Plan—Varied Learning Activities

### Connect with Life

1. After welcoming the class and opening with prayer, point to the heading you've written on the board that reads "Figures of Speech." State that the term "figure of speech" refers to an expression, as a metaphor or simile, that uses words in a nonliteral or unusual sense to add vividness or beauty to a description. Give some examples of figures of speech ("My love is a red, red rose"; "You are the salt of the earth"; "Kill the fatted calf"; "Faith as small as a mustard seed"; "The mark of Cain"; "Eat, drink, and be merry"; "Don't hide your light under a bushel"; etc.). Include some colloquial figures of speech your class members are familiar with. Invite class members to provide examples of their favorite figures of speech. You may want to ask: *What were some figures of speech your parents or teachers used?*

### Guide Bible Study

2. Explain that in today's Scripture text we find four figures of speech that Jesus used to communicate his mission and his identity. Write the words "Spiritual Blindness" on the board. State, *Before we read the text for today, each of you share with the person next to you what you think this figure of speech means.* Allow a few minutes for this exchange.

3. Have the learners open their Bibles to John 9:1–7. Share background information on the passage (use "Understanding the Context" in this *Teaching Guide* for this information). Enlist someone to read the passage aloud while class members listen for the details of the situation.

4. Help the class explore the passage by asking questions like these:
   - Who are the main characters in this event?
   - What do you think prompted the disciples' question?
   - What figure of speech did Jesus use in this passage in referring to himself? ("the light of the world")
   - Given the context, why is this an appropriate figure of speech to use?
   - What do you think Jesus was trying to communicate in using this figure of speech?
   - How does Jesus' figure of speech of being the light of the world relate to your understanding of "spiritual blindness"?

   Conclude this section by suggesting that in 9:39–41 Jesus provided an interpretation of his healing the blind man by talking about spiritual blindness. Read these verses aloud and provide an interpretation based on "The Need for Spiritual Vision" in the *Study Guide.* Encourage discussion and exploration by inviting the class to summarize what they think Jesus was saying.

5. Inform the class that they will examine three more figures of speech used by Jesus. Remind the class of the definition of a figure of speech (see step 1). Invite members to work in pairs and identify the figures of speech found in 10:1–18 (verses 1–6, the sheepfold; verses 7–10, the door; and verses 11–18, the Good Shepherd). Give the pairs enough time to find the figures of speech; list them on the board as members share their findings. Encourage the class to interpret what Jesus was trying to communicate by using the figures of speech. Use the information in the *Study Guide* to help members to expand, clarify, and fine-tune their interpretations.

## Encourage Application

6. Reserve at least twenty minutes for the "Encourage Application" portion of this lesson, apportioning it as indicated in steps 6 and 7.

Instruct the class to form groups of three or four people (but no more than four). Refer to questions 2–6 in the "Questions" section of the *Study Guide.* Allow about twelve minutes for this activity. Instruct groups that they may choose to start with any question but to be sure to answer question 6. Give a signal when only two minutes remain for group work so that groups will be sure to focus on question 6 if they have not done so.

7.  Call time at least eight minutes before you need to conclude the session. Invite responses on the questions, moving from one group to the next on each question.

8.  Give attention to verse 19. Invite questions or comments on why the Jews were divided. Invite the class to close their eyes and ask themselves this question: *We couldn't be blind, could we?* Close with prayer.

## Teaching Plan—Lecture and Questions

### Connect with Life

1.  Welcome the class and open the session with prayer. Use the "Figures of Speech" activity found in step 1 of "Teaching Plan—Varied Learning Activities." This step will help highlight the use of the literary device in the text.

### Guide Bible Study

2.  Using the following outline as a focal point (write it on the chalkboard or display on a poster), give the class an overview of the lesson:

---

### The Good Shepherd and Human Blindness
   I. Jesus Heals the Blind Man (9:1–7)
  II. The Need for Spiritual Vision (9:39–41)
 III. Figures of Speech
     A. The Sheepfold (10:1–6)
     B. The Door (10:7–10)
     C. The Good Shepherd (10:11–18)
 IV. Division Among the People (10:19)

---

3. Enlist a volunteer to read John 9:1–7 aloud. Assign three members to listen for the following items and report the following after the reading: (1) the characters in the story; (2) the events; (3) the figure of speech used by Jesus. At the conclusion of the reading, have the three report their findings. Summarize and interpret the passage, using information from the *Study Guide* and from "Bible Comments" in this *Teaching Guide*.

4. Lead the class in exploring 9:1–7 through a guided discussion. Use questions like the following:
   - What do you think prompted the disciples' question about sin and blindness?
   - What figure of speech did Jesus use in this passage? ("the light of the world")
   - Given the context, why is this an appropriate figure of speech to use?
   - How does Jesus' figure of speech of being the light of the world relate to your understanding of spiritual blindness?
   - What might be some characteristics of a spiritually blind person?
   - How can a person know when he or she is spiritually blind?

5. Refer to point II on the focal outline and invite the class to see what Jesus had to say about spiritual blindness and spiritual seeing. Read 9:39–41 aloud. Explain that the disciples often complained about Jesus' "hard sayings." Challenge the class members to interpret the hard saying found in verse 39. Refer to ideas in "The Need for Spiritual Vision" in the *Study Guide*.

6. Refer to point III on the outline and call attention to the three figures of speech that Jesus used to identify his work and person: (1) the sheepfold in 10:1–6; (2) the door in 10:7–10; and (3) the Good Shepherd in 10:11–18. Divide the room into two sides (class members can remain in their seats). Assign one side of the room the topic "Mission" and the second side the topic "Person." Have each side take turns suggesting how Jesus' figures of speech relate to their topic. List their responses on the board. When you have at least six responses from each side, use the list, the information from the *Study Guide*, and the information on these verses in this *Teaching Guide* to summarize how Jesus used these figures of speech to communicate his mission and identity.

## Encourage Application

7. Direct the learners to read 9:40–41. Point out how the text described the spiritual blindness of the Pharisees. Ask, *What are some ways in which people can be spiritually blind? Is there a cure for spiritual blindness? What is it?*

8. Challenge the class to apply the lesson by closing their eyes and asking themselves silently the question the Pharisees asked (9:40): "Are we blind too?" After a few moments, invite members to remain with their eyes closed, but to ask, in turn, out loud, the question, *Am I blind too?* Pause for a few moments after the last person has said the phrase. Then close in prayer, asking God to help us when we are spiritually blind.

## Focal Text

John 11:14–44, 47–53

## Background

John 11:1–54

## Main Idea

Jesus challenges us to respond to him as the One who offers and is the resurrection and the life.

## Question to Explore

Do you believe this?

## Teaching Aim

To lead the class to respond to Jesus as the One who offers and is the resurrection and the life

## Lesson Eight

# The Resurrection and the Life

## BIBLE COMMENTS

### Understanding the Context

The raising of Lazarus from the dead was the most dramatic and climactic of all of Jesus' miracles. It was dramatic in the sense that Lazarus had been dead for four days (John 11:17), unlike the raising of the daughter of Jairus (Mark 5:22–43) and of the son of a widow (Luke 7:12–15). It was climactic in that it precipitated the signing of Jesus' death warrant by the Jewish council.

In John 11:1–13 we are introduced to the characters, and the stage is set for the raising of Lazarus. Jesus was in Perea, on the east side of Jordan, when he received the message of Lazarus' illness (John 10:40; 11:3).

We have no extensive record of Jesus' relationship with the family of Mary, Martha, and Lazarus. The first recorded encounter is with the sisters in their home in Bethany (Luke 10:38–42). John distinguishes this Mary from the others by stating that she was "the same one who poured perfume on the Lord and wiped his feet with her hair" (John 11:2).

The first response of Jesus to the message that Lazarus was sick was to tell his disciples that the final outcome of his sickness would not be death. This miracle was to be a means to glorify God and in turn bring glory to the Son as well. No explanation is given as to why Jesus delayed in returning to Judea.

When Jesus announced that he would return, the disciples tried to dissuade him for fear of his life (11:8). He contrasted light and darkness as an analogy (11:9). He said one may walk in the light and avoid the stumbling blocks whereas at night one may stumble and fall. He applied light to the time for him to remain on earth and accomplish the Father's will. He knew that until then no harm would come to him. Earlier Jesus had said, "As long as it is day, we must do the work of him who sent me. Night is coming, when no one can work" (9:4).

The Gospel of John recalls Jesus' dialogue with his disciples (11:1–17). It then relates Jesus' conversation with Martha (11:18–28) and with Mary (11:29–33). The raising of Lazarus is the graphic description of an eyewitness (11:34–43). The remaining verses report the response of the Jews and the decision of the council to sign Jesus' death warrant (11:44–54).

## Interpreting the Scriptures

### A Dangerous Return to Judea (11:14–16)

**11:14.** Jesus' declaration that Lazarus was dead was necessary because the disciples misunderstood what Jesus meant when he said that Lazarus was asleep (11:11). Sleep was often used in the New Testament to describe death (see Matthew 9:24; Acts 7:60; 1 Thessalonians 4:13).

**11:15.** The implication is that had Jesus been present when Lazarus became ill, Jesus would have healed him. Inasmuch as bringing back to life a person who had been dead for four days was such an impressive miracle, Jesus saw Lazarus' death as an opportunity to increase the faith of the disciples and manifest the glory of God.

**11:16.** When Jesus declared he was returning to Judea (11:7), the disciples feared for Jesus' life, and likely for their own. Thomas, however, showed both courage and loyalty when he declared that they should go with Jesus, even if it meant death.

UNIT THREE: The Time Has Come

## Resurrection Comfort (11:17–27)

**11:17.** It probably took the messenger one day to deliver the message of Lazarus' sickness to Jesus. Jesus delayed two days. Then he returned on the fourth day to find that Lazarus had been in the tomb four days.

**11:18–19.** The fact that Bethany was less than two miles from Jerusalem may imply that many of the mourners were prominent Jews from Jerusalem. These mourners had remained friends with, or at least continued to respect, Mary, Martha, and Lazarus, even though the three had become followers of Jesus. The Jewish custom, as in our culture, was to share in the sorrow of a family who has lost a loved one. Unlike our custom, the mourners came and remained for long periods of time. The mourners could also have been professional mourners.

**11:20.** The Scripture does not indicate why Martha, on hearing that Jesus was near, ran to meet him while Mary remained in the house. It may be that she simply preferred to talk with Jesus in private.

**11:21–22.** Martha's statement was an affirmation of faith, not a rebuke. She had no doubt that Lazarus would not have died had Jesus been present. We are reminded of the faith of the mother of Jesus at the wedding in Cana when she told the servants, "Do whatever he tells you" (2:5). The faith of the centurion is another example. When Jesus agreed to go to his house and heal his servant, the centurion said, "Just say the word, and my servant will be healed" (Matt. 8:8). Martha's faith allowed her to believe that God would faithfully answer any prayer offered by Jesus, including the raising of her brother from the dead. She recognized that Jesus' power came from God. She likely knew of the restoration of Jairus's daughter and the son of the widow of Nain. Such knowledge helped fortify her faith.

**11:23–24.** In response to Jesus' statement that Lazarus would "rise again," Martha declared her belief in the resurrection at the last day. From whence came this belief? The view of the resurrection in the Old Testament is rather vague (see Job 19:25–27). Although the Sadducees refused to believe in the resurrection, the Pharisees held that view. Too, since Jesus was often in the family home, Martha may have learned of the resurrection from Jesus. Previously he had referred to the resurrection at the last day (John 6:39).

**11:25–26.** Jesus claimed to be "the resurrection and the life." This life and resurrection is for all who believe. There are no other exclusions. The promise is clear: "Whoever believes in him shall not perish but have eternal life" (John 3:16).

In my years as pastor, I found no Scripture that spoke greater comfort to the bereaved than Jesus' statement in these verses. Surely Jesus did not mean that those who believe will not experience death. He uttered these words in the presence of physical death. Christ was speaking of spiritual life. He is saying that death is not the end of life but the beginning of real life, life that knows no end.

**11:27.** The word "believe" acknowledges soul competence, the ability of "whosoever will" to approach the throne of grace, ask forgiveness, and receive life that never ends. When Jesus asked Martha whether she believed, her response acknowledged not only her belief in what Jesus had said but also in who Jesus was—the Christ, the Son of God, and the Coming One. Her answer was in response to the question of Jesus in verse 25, "Do you believe this?" In this day of doubt, this may be a good question for all of us.

### Sympathizing Comfort (11:28–37)

**11:28–30.** After Jesus' conversation with Martha, Jesus asked to see Mary. Just as Martha had had a private conversation with Jesus, apart from the unbelieving Jews, she desired the same for Mary. She spoke to her sister privately. Jesus also desired privacy, having remained outside the city. Mary used the name "Teacher" for Jesus, which seems to have been the title by which they usually addressed him.

**11:31–32.** When Mary saw Jesus, she fell at his feet and exclaimed the words Martha also had used (11:21). Undoubtedly the sisters had discussed this certainty before. Her statement was also an affirmation of her faith. Mary began to weep, as did those who accompanied her.

**11:33.** At this sight Jesus was "deeply moved in spirit and troubled." The Greek word translated "deeply moved" literally means *to snort*. In this setting the word could indicate that Jesus was expressing both grief and anger. His grief was real. It could be that Jesus was also angry at the hypocritical mourners who showed sympathy on the outside but felt none on the inside. In my pastoral experience I have witnessed such a mixture of emotion. The loved one may be angry at God, or the doctor, or the deceased for dying and leaving him or her to handle life and its responsibilities alone.

Standing in the presence of death and its accompanying sorrow in the life of his dear friends, Jesus was deeply moved. He is our high priest who is able to sympathize with us in our weaknesses (Hebrews 4:15).

**11:34–35.** "Jesus wept" is the shortest verse in the Bible, but these two words reveal the very heart of God. Does it seem strange that Jesus would weep, having told his disciples that he was going to awake Lazarus? Revealed here is the human side of the incarnate Christ. We also get a glimpse of how much God cares for us. Jesus wept because he loved Lazarus.

**11:36–37.** Even the Jews observed Jesus' tears as an expression of love. However, some were puzzled that having made the blind man see (John 9:6–7), Jesus did not prevent Lazarus' death.

## The Answered Prayer (11:38–44)

**11:38.** As Jesus approached the tomb, he was again greatly moved. The tomb likely was cave-like, dug into the side of the mountain, with a huge stone across the entrance. The stone was rolled through a trough to its resting place.

**11:39–40.** It did not take a miracle to roll away the stone; therefore, Jesus asked someone else to remove it. Martha's hesitation to have the tomb opened issued out of two concerns. First, Lazarus had not been embalmed and had been dead four days. The odor would be unbearable. Second, she may have wavered momentarily in her faith that Jesus would raise her brother from the dead. Jesus asked, "Did I not tell you that if you believed, you would see the glory of God?" She objected no more.

**11:41.** The stone was rolled away, and Jesus prayed. His prayer indicated that previously he had received from the Father the promise of power to raise Lazarus from the dead. Actually, Jesus' prayer was not a petition to God but was said aloud that the witnesses might know that God had sent him and that all his miracles were according to the will and power of God.

**11:42–44.** Then Jesus shouted, "Lazarus, come out," and he did. Jesus then asked someone to remove the grave clothes.

There is a distinct difference between the resurrection of Lazarus and the resurrection of Jesus. Lazarus arose to die again. Jesus arose never to die again. Jesus' resurrection is the guarantee of our resurrection. "But Christ has indeed been raised from the dead, the first fruits of those who have fallen asleep" (1 Corinthians 15:20). Jesus' resurrection from the dead assures us of our resurrection at the last day.

## Death Warrant Signed (11:45–53)

**11:44–48.** Many of those who followed Mary to the tomb believed. Some, however, did not. They went immediately to the Pharisees to report what they had seen. So disturbed by what they had heard, the Jewish leaders called a meeting of the Sanhedrin. Although they might not have accepted the miracles of Jesus as a work of God, they did acknowledge the truth of them. Their fear was that, left alone, Jesus would win such a following that Rome would become disturbed. This might result in the loss of power and prestige that the Sanhedrin had.

**11:49–52.** Caiaphas, the high priest in this momentous year, spoke a prophetic word when he said that it was better that one man die for the nation than that the entire nation be destroyed. John made a prophetic application of the statement. To him it meant that Jesus would die for the Jewish nation but also for the whole world—Jews and Gentiles. Jesus would fulfill the words he spoke about having other sheep not of this fold. There would be one flock and one shepherd (10:16).

**11:53.** The hostility against Jesus had been growing steadily (10:31, 39). It came to a boiling point when Caiaphas declared that every effort must be made to silence Jesus. Thus the plan to kill Jesus was set in motion.

## Focusing on the Meaning

*Resurrection now.* Consider Jesus as the resurrection and the life. Think not only of Jesus' resurrection but also of the promise of the resurrection of those who believe in him as well as of the resurrection that comes in this present life. Ephesians 2:1 tells us that we are all dead in our "transgressions and sins," but "God raised us up with Christ" (Eph. 2:6).

*God's timetable.* On receiving the message of Lazarus' sickness, Jesus did not return to Bethany immediately. God works on his timetable, not ours. We often become impatient that God does not respond to our prayers immediately. If we trust God to respond in God's own time, then we will "know that in all things God works for the good of those who love him" (Romans 8:28).

*Crisis.* The death of Lazarus produced a crisis. The crisis for Jesus was returning to a hostile environment. The crisis for Mary and Martha was a crisis of faith. In such a moment we may turn to God or away from God. The two sisters chose to turn in faith to God. Their choice produced a situation in which witnesses saw the "glory of God" (John 11:40). Thus a crisis can stretch our faith and enable us to grow spiritually.

*Refuge and restoration.* The home of Mary, Martha, and Lazarus was a place of refuge and restoration for Jesus. It was here Jesus could withdraw for comfort and appreciation. We all need such a place. It may be a place of solitude in the beauty of nature. It may be some trusted friend with whom we may share in confidence and trust.

*Doing what we can.* A miracle was needed to raise Lazarus from the dead but not to roll away the stone. Jesus asked others to do that. Jesus does not do for us what we can do for ourselves. Some of our prayers can be answered by ourselves.

*Grief and faith.* From the experience of Mary and Martha, whom Jesus loved, we see that grief is a part of life even for people of faith. Having faith in God and expressing grief at the loss of a loved one are not incompatible.

# TEACHING PLANS

## Teaching Plan—Varied Learning Activities

### Connect with Life

1. After welcoming the class and opening with prayer, lead the class members in the following opening activity. Write *P.O.V.* on the board. Ask, *What does "P.O.V." stand for?* ("Point of View"). *Why do you think people have so many different points of view of any given subject?* Allow members to share their opinions.

2. To illustrate "point of view" and to introduce the lesson, tell the classic story of the five blind men and the elephant. Tell the story dramatically so that it's an enjoyable experience for the class. In the story, five blind men decide to investigate the strange animal they've

heard about. Each man is able to touch and feel only one part of the elephant. They thus arrive at their individual conclusions about this mysterious creature. The man who feels the trunk believes that the elephant is like a big snake. The man who feels the ear believes that the elephant is like a huge, veined fan. The man who feels the side believes that the elephant is like a huge, breathing wall. The man who feels the legs believes that the elephant is like the trunk of a tree. The man who feels the tail believes that the elephant is like a long, thin, bristly porcupine.

When you complete the story, ask, *Is it possible for any of us to be totally objective? Why or why not?* Allow time for responses.

## Guide Bible Study

3. Explain that today's Bible lesson shows that people had different points of view about Jesus even when he revealed his power and person most clearly. Explain that in today's lesson different points of view brought different responses from people about their relationship to Jesus.

> ### The Resurrection and the Life
> I. Jesus Returns to Bethany (11:14–16)
> II. Jesus Arrives at Bethany and Meets Martha (11:17–27)
> III. Mary Comes to Jesus (11:28–37)
> IV. Jesus Raises Lazarus (11:37–44)
> V. Jewish Authorities Plot Against Jesus (11:47–53)

4. Present an overview of the Bible passage by using the outline found in the *Study Guide.* Posting the outline on the board or on a poster will help your class stay on track as you explore the passage. Finish your overview by stating that as we study the passage today the focus will be on discovering several responses to Jesus and finally on examining our personal response to Jesus.

5. Summarize the circumstances surrounding the news of Lazarus' sickness and death in 11:1–13. Tell the class to listen for the responses concerning Jesus in this first reading (sisters, disciples).

Enlist a volunteer to read 11:14–37 aloud. Encourage the class to share observations about the passage.

6. Form the class into three study groups. Assign the following and allow three to five minutes for this activity:
   - *Group A: John 11:14–16.* What was Thomas' response to Jesus? How did Thomas' response reflect his belief in Jesus as "the resurrection and the life"?
   - *Group B: John 11:17–27.* What was Martha's response to Jesus? How did Martha's response reflect her belief in Jesus as "the resurrection and the life"?
   - *Group C: John 11:28–37.* What was Mary's response to Jesus? How did Mary's response reflect her belief in Jesus as "the resurrection and the life"?

7. Invite groups to report. Then encourage the class to look at the next response to Jesus as the resurrection and the life. Read 11:38–44 aloud. Ask, *What was Lazarus' response to Jesus as the resurrection and the life?* Lead the class to explore the meaning of resurrection and life. Write on the board: *Lazarus, Jesus, Us.* Ask, *How is resurrection the same and different for each of these?* Share information as needed from "Bible Comments" on 11:42–44 in this *Teaching Guide.*

## Encourage Application

8. State that there is one more response we need to look at in the passage found in 11:47–53. Ask a volunteer to read 11:47–53 aloud. Then ask, *What was the response of the Jewish authorities to Jesus as the resurrection and the life? Would you have expected this response? What would have been a more logical response?* Point out how the raising of Lazarus and the willful response of the chief priests and Pharisees represents a turning point in the Gospel of John.

9. Summarize the responses of Thomas, Martha, Mary, Lazarus, and the Jews. Then invite the class to consider their own response to Jesus as the resurrection and the life. Distribute slips of paper or 3" x 5" index cards and challenge the class to make an individual response to these two elements: (1) "My response to Jesus as the resurrection and the life in my living is . . . ."; (2) "My response to Jesus as the resurrection and the life in my dying is . . . ." Close the class with prayer.

## Teaching Plan—Lecture and Questions

### Connect with Life

1. After welcoming the class and opening with prayer, lead the class in the following opening activity. Ask the class whether they remember learning about the life cycle of a butterfly. Ask, *What is the process associated with the life cycle of a butterfly called?* (Answer: Metamorphosis.) Write the word on the board. Invite the class to pretend that a child has found a caterpillar and asks you to explain the process of how it will become a butterfly. Lead the class to describe the process of metamorphosis from beginning to end. Challenge them to recall the correct terms for all stages and for the process by asking, *And what is that called? What is the correct term for that?* As the class describes the process, write it on the board or on a flipchart. (Here is the process: a. The adult female is fertilized. b. The female lays eggs. c. A caterpillar hatches from egg as larva. d. The caterpillar grows to full size and begins hibernation. e. The caterpillar develops a pupal case for protection. f. The pupa or chrysalis undergoes metamorphosis. g. Adult butterfly emerges.)

   Your class's list does not have to look exactly like the above, but challenge the class to get all of the steps in order, with the correct terms. Give clues as needed.

2. Explain that today's Bible passage deals with life, death, and resurrection. Ask, *What is the difference between "metamorphosis" and "resurrection"?* Allow the class time to compare and contrast these terms.

### Guide Bible Study

3. Provide a preview of the Bible study passage for today by going over the outline you've written on the board or provided on a poster.

4. Summarize the circumstances surrounding the news of Lazarus' sickness and death in 11:1–13. Read 11:14–53 aloud in its entirety as members follow in their Bibles.

5. Lead members to explore the passage by using the outline. Guide discussion by asking questions like those that follow. Use the

JOHN: So That You May Believe—Teaching Guide

material in the *Study Guide* and in "Bible Comments" in this *Teaching Guide* to provide information, clarification, interpretation, and explanation during the discussion.

I. Jesus Returns to Bethany (11:14–16)
- What do you think was for the "sake" of the disciples?
- Why did Thomas make such a foreboding statement?
- If you were standing next to Thomas when he made that statement, what would you say to him?

II. Jesus Arrives at Bethany and Meets Martha (11:17–27)
- How did Martha respond to Jesus as the resurrection and the life?
- Do Martha's statements of grief indicate a strong faith or a lack of faith?
- What is the "I am" statement that Jesus makes in this passage?
- How do you interpret Jesus' declaration that he is "the resurrection and the life"?

III. Mary Comes to Jesus (11:28–37)
- How do you interpret the fact that Mary's first response was almost identical to Martha's?
- How do you interpret John's depiction of Jesus' weeping?
- How do you answer the question in verse 37?

IV. Jesus Raises Lazarus (11:37–44)
- How does this sign confirm that Jesus is the "resurrection and the life"?
- Is Lazarus' resurrection the same or different from Jesus' resurrection?
- Is Lazarus' resurrection the same or different from the resurrection that we hope for?

V. Jewish Authorities Plot Against Jesus (11:47–53)
- Do you find something astounding about the response of the authorities? What?
- What do you think makes us make choices against all evidence to the contrary?
- How does John indicate a shift in the narrative in relation to the response of the authorities?

## Encourage Application

6. Remind the class of the opening activity about metamorphosis. Recall that in that step they were asked to compare and contrast the concepts of "metamorphosis" and "resurrection." Lead the class to come up with a definition of "resurrection." Allow the class to work together to come up with a definition that satisfies all members. (Keep the definition simple, like, *Resurrection means rising from the dead, or coming back to life.*) Then ask: *(1) What does it mean that Jesus is the resurrection and the life in my living? (2) What does it mean that Jesus is the resurrection and the life in my dying?* Allow sufficient time for this application step, and then close in prayer.

## Main Idea

Jesus offered himself to draw all people—including us—to him, challenging us to decide whether we will follow him.

## Question to Explore

What does Jesus' offer of himself 2000 years ago mean for you today?

## Teaching Aim

To lead the class to describe the significance for their lives of Jesus' offering himself to draw all people to him

## UNIT THREE

### The Time Has Come

# Lesson Nine

# The Hour Has Come

## BIBLE COMMENTS

### Understanding the Context

After Jesus' raising of Lazarus from the dead, the Jewish leaders had decided that Jesus had to be stopped by taking his life (11:53). Jesus thus had withdrawn from public ministry (11:54). John 11:55–56 tells of the approaching Passover and the questioning among the people as to whether Jesus would attend. Verse 57 reminds us of the danger Jesus faced if he did indeed come to the Passover.

John 12:1 indicates that in spite of the danger, Jesus was on his way to the Passover and drawing near to Jerusalem. The first narrative in John 12 has its setting in Bethany, six days prior to Pentecost, where Jesus was being honored at a supper (12:1–11). Martha was serving the meal. Lazarus, brother to Martha and Mary, was present. Mary opened a bottle of expensive perfume, anointed the feet of Jesus, and wiped his feet with her hair. Although Mary did not understand the full significance of what she had done, Jesus indicated that she had anointed him for his burial. Many Jews were present at this supper to see both Jesus and Lazarus, whose miraculous resurrection had brought many of them to believe on Jesus. The chief priests, who had determined to do away with Jesus, also decided they must do away with Lazarus.

The second narrative (12:12–19) describes Christ's triumphal entry into Jerusalem. The crowd that waved palm branches consisted of those who had accompanied Jesus from Bethany as well as the pilgrims who had come from outside of Jerusalem for the Passover. They cried "Hosanna," applauding Jesus as the one who had come to deliver the nation from Roman rule. The fact that Jesus came riding on a donkey, rather than a horse, indicated that he was a messenger of peace, a fulfillment of Zechariah 9:9. Jesus' riding on a donkey was a parable of the kind of King he was. Even the disciples did not realize the significance of this event until after Christ's death and resurrection. The Jews who had witnessed the resurrection of Lazarus continued to share what they had seen and heard. This response frustrated the Pharisees with their inability to halt the defection. To them, "the whole world" was turning to Jesus.

John 12:20–22 indicates the wideness of the world that was coming to Jesus. The Greeks symbolized the world beyond the Jewish people. After Jesus' discourse in 12:23–36 occurs a statement about the Jews' rejection of Jesus (12:37–43; see 1:11). The closing verses of the chapter, 12:44–50, provide a summary of the thrust of Jesus' message and ministry to this point and call for decision about Jesus.


## Interpreting the Scriptures


### The Pilgrims' Interest in Jesus (11:55–57)

**11:55.** The third and last Passover during Jesus' earthly ministry was approaching. Many of the Jews came from the country outside Jerusalem. They came early for the purification ritual, knowing they could have become contaminated along the way by touching a dead animal or even coming in contact with certain foreigners. They preferred to do their ceremonial cleansing in the temple after they arrived in the Holy City.

**11:56–57.** Having heard about the miraculous raising of Lazarus from the dead, these Passover pilgrims were eager to see Jesus. However, because of the command of the Pharisees that anyone who saw Jesus was to report it, they wondered whether he would dare show up for the Feast.

Likely they were not aware that the Pharisees' plan was to put Jesus to death rather than simply arrest him.

## The Greeks' Request and Jesus' Response (12:20–33)

**12:20–22.** Since John's Gospel has the Gentiles in mind, it is little wonder this event is included. These Greeks were likely proselytes to the Jewish faith. Being serious seekers after the truth, they sought out Philip with the request to see Jesus. Why Philip? Possibly because he had a Greek name and was from Bethsaida, a city with many Greek inhabitants. Philip sought the counsel of Andrew. Because of the hostile attitude toward the Gentiles, Philip may have been fearful of the reaction of the Pharisees if Jesus met with these Greeks.

**12:23.** When Philip and Andrew told Jesus of the request by the Greeks, he was deeply moved and responded with a most significant discourse. The coming of these Gentiles prompted Jesus to exclaim, "The hour has come for the Son of Man to be glorified" (12:23). On three occasions prior to this incident, Jesus had said that his hour or time had not yet come (John 2:4; 7:30; 8:20). The "hour" referred to Jesus' death. His glorification included his death, resurrection, exaltation, and return to the Father.

**12:24.** Once again Jesus used the realm of nature to set forth a spiritual truth—that life comes through death (12:24). If a grain of wheat is to multiply itself, it must be buried in the ground and die. Jesus applied this analogy to himself.

**12:25–26.** The principle of kingdom service is laid down in these verses (see also Matthew 16:25; Mark 8:35). Jesus had said, "A student is not above his teacher, nor a servant above his master" (Matt. 10:25). Thus Jesus' followers must also die to self that they may be productive servants. Life is gained by losing it and lost by holding on to it. This was the testimony of Paul, who for the love of Christ testified of having "lost all things . . . that I may gain Christ" (Philippians 3:8).

We are not only to deny self, but also we are to accept Jesus' principles and pattern for our lives. The result of such commitment is eternal life, which includes a quality of life here and now and eternal life in glory. The Father will honor those who serve Christ. The promise is that we will be "heirs of God and co-heirs with Christ, if indeed we share in his sufferings in order that we may also share in his glory" (Romans 8:17).

**12:27.** Once again we see the humanity of Jesus. We saw it as he wept at the grave of Lazarus (11:35). The coming of the Greeks, signifying Jesus' redemptive ministry to the whole world, brought Jesus once again to the agony of the cross. The cry of Jesus is translated as a question, "What shall I say? 'Father save me from this hour?'" No one would want to die on a cross or even at so young an age. As in Gethsemane, Jesus followed his petition with an affirmation of his faithfulness to his mission (see Matt. 26:39).

**12:28.** Jesus then prayed, "Father glorify your name!" The response was a voice from heaven indicating that God had glorified God's name in the past and would do it again. God was glorified by the ministry of Christ and would soon be glorified by Christ's death and resurrection.

**12:29–30.** Some of the crowd recognized the voice as coming from heaven although they did not understand the words. Jesus affirmed their belief when he told them that the voice was for their benefit, not his.

**12:31.** Christ's death would bring judgment on the sinful world and break the rule of Satan in the hearts of those who believe. The cross has a twofold message. It stands as the greatest condemnation of sin, but it also symbolizes the power of Christ to provide release and redemption from sin.

**12:32–33.** This is the third time the Gospel of John speaks of Jesus being "lifted up" (3:14; 8:28). The immediate meaning of Christ being "lifted up" is his death on the cross. It also refers to his exaltation (Phil. 2:9–11). The result of Jesus' crucifixion is that he will "draw all men to" himself, a reference to the universal scope of Jesus' redemptive power.

### The Son of Man and the Sons of Light (12:34–36).

**12:34.** When Jesus indicated he would die on a cross—"be lifted up"—the crowd stood in disbelief. They could not envision the Son of Man on a cross. From the Hebrew Scriptures, they had deduced that the Messiah would reign forever on the earth. Their concept of the Son of Man was an invincible Conqueror who would head an everlasting kingdom. Thus they asked, "Who is this 'Son of Man'?" That is, what relationship does a crucified Son of Man have to the Messiah?

**12:35–36a.** Jesus seems to have ignored their question. Rather he made one last appeal to them to come to the truth. He had used the analogy of light earlier as the limited time for him to complete his earthly ministry (9:4). He now used light to symbolize the short time the Jews had to accept him as Savior before his death and ascension.

Darkness is the symbol of evil. Jesus encouraged his followers to walk in the light while it is available, before darkness overtook them. This was an urgent appeal to forsake the darkness of unbelief and put their trust in the light of God's truth. In doing so, they would become "sons of light," that is, witnesses of Jesus as the Light.

**12:36b–37.** Having concluded his public ministry, Jesus withdrew. He dedicated his remaining time to his inner circle of true believers.

## The Word, Our Salvation or Our Condemnation (12:44–50)

Chapter 12 is brought to a close by a summary of Jesus' message and ministry, including the person of Jesus and his relation to the Father.

**12:44–45.** Jesus said that to believe in him is to believe also in the Father, the One who sent him. Jesus and the Father are one. When we look at Jesus, we see the Father also.

**12:46.** Jesus is the Light of the world, who dispels the darkness of sin that covers the world. So powerful is the Light that the darkness cannot extinguish it (see 1:5).

**12:47–48.** Jesus made it clear that "God did not send his Son into the world to condemn the world, but to save the world through him" (John 3:17). He came as Savior, not as judge. We condemn ourselves, however, by rejecting Jesus. The "last day" refers to the final judgment.

**12:49–50.** Jesus' obedience to the Father's will included speaking the words the Father gave him.

## Focusing on the Meaning

*The sin of self-centeredness.* Jesus condemned self-centeredness (12:25a). Selfishness is a sin.

*Count the cost.* Christ does not lead us to follow him blindly. There is a price to pay (12:25). In Luke 14:26–33, Jesus tells us that before following him, we must count the cost.

*Believe=commit.* The word *believe* means *commit.* Let me illustrate. I believe in my car. I commit myself to it daily. I believe in the airplane. Often I board an airplane, committing myself to the safety of the plane and the competence of the pilots. I do not believe in the space ship. I am not about to climb in one and ride it into space. The difference is commitment. To believe in Jesus we must commit ourselves completely to him.

*Introducing people to Jesus.* While eating in a restaurant, I noticed that Pat Neff, former governor of Texas, was seated at a table near me. Overhearing a conversation at another table, I became aware of the presence of the present governor of New Mexico. Boldly, I introduced the governor of New Mexico to the former governor of Texas without knowing either one of them. However, to introduce someone to Jesus, one must know him personally, as did Philip and Andrew.

*Before it is too late.* In 12:35–36a Jesus stressed the urgency of trusting in him before it is too late. We should have a sense of urgency about sharing the gospel with the unsaved before it is too late for both them and us.

*Giving life through dying.* One of my favorite sights in Olympic National Forest in Washington is the "nurse tree." Years ago some of the giant trees fell and began to decay. Seeds from other trees fell into the cavities of a rotting tree where they sprouted and found nourishment. As many as six trees have been given life by the dead tree.

# TEACHING PLANS

## Teaching Plan—Varied Learning Activities

### Connect with Life

1. Invite the class to guess the answer to the riddles you are about to share, and state that the one who guesses the most riddles correctly wins. (If someone asks, *Wins what?* answer, *Just wins!*). In addition to or instead of the riddles that follow, you may wish to use some of your favorite riddles. Be sure, however, that the riddles relate to time in some way.

## Riddles

Q. What is the cheapest time to call friends long distance?
A. When they are not home.

Q. What time is it when a monkey steals your watch?
A. Time to get a new watch.

Q. Why did the little girl throw her clock out the window?
A. She wanted to see time fly.

Q. What time do you go to the dentist?
A. Tooth Hurty.

Q. What time is it when ten cats chase a mouse?
A. Ten after one.

Q. What is coming but never arrives?
A. Tomorrow.

Q. What dog keeps the best time?
A. A watch dog.

Q. When is the best time to have lunch?
A. After breakfast.

Q. What time is it when an elephant sits on your fence?
A. Time to get a new fence.

2. Have fun with this introductory exercise. When you finish all of the riddles, ask, *What did all these riddles have in common?* (They all have to do with time.) Then state that you have one more riddle that has to do with today's lesson and invite the class to see whether they can answer this one: *What time was it when Philip brought the Greeks to Jesus?* (It was the time when the hour had come.) If someone answers correctly, use the response as a way to review or introduce the literary use of "the hour" in the Gospel of John. Use information in the comments on 12:23 in this *Teaching Guide.* If no one guesses the riddle correctly, write the phrase "the hour has come" on the board and tell the class that you will soon study what that riddle means.

## Guide Bible Study

3. Explain that in today's Bible lesson the "riddle" that John has been teasing his readers with, that Jesus' "hour has not yet come," is finally answered. Overview the lesson by using as an outline the headings found in the *Study Guide*. Write the outline on the board or make a poster. Explain that in today's text the Gospel of John shows Jesus' understanding of his mission and demonstrates Jesus' clear intent to follow God's will for his life—to offer himself so as to draw people to himself.

4. Direct the class to read John 11:55–57. Point out that these verses provide the dramatic backdrop for the events to follow. Use the *Study Guide* and the comments on these verses in this *Teaching Guide* to provide information to help the class interpret the passage. Give attention to (a) Passover as a backdrop for the events and (b) the response of the chief priests and Pharisees to Jesus.

5. Lead the class to form at least two interpretation groups and use the group instructions that follow to guide their interpretation of the passage. Have six or fewer people in each group. Form additional groups with duplicate assignments if attendance is larger than twelve. Allow about ten minutes for group work.

    *Group A—John 12:20–37.* First, choose a timekeeper and prompter to help keep your group on task. Read John 12:20–37, and respond to the following questions. Be prepared to share your group's conclusions.

    (1) Begin your study by answering these basic interpretation questions based on your reading: *Who, What, When, Where, and How.*

    (2) Identify and interpret unusual, important, or unique words and phrases in the passage. Use the *Study Guide* for assistance.

    (3) Interpret the meaning of the following:

        a. The Greeks coming to see Jesus

        b. Jesus' use of the phrase "the hour has come"

        c. Jesus' use of the metaphor of the grain of wheat

    *Group B—John 12:44–50.* First, choose a timekeeper and prompter to help keep your group on task. Read John 12:44–50, and respond to the following questions. Be prepared to share your group's conclusions.

    (1) Begin your study by answering these basic interpretation questions based on your reading: *Who, What, When, Where, and How.*

    (2) Identify and interpret unusual, important, or unique words and phrases in the passage. Use the *Study Guide* for assistance.

    (3) Interpret the meaning of the following:

        a. Jesus' statements concerning belief in him and belief in God.

        b. Jesus' statement about judgment

        c. Jesus' relationship with the Father

6. When you call the groups to report on their findings, use their observations to explore the passage. Do this by asking probing questions, asking for clarification, expanding on their responses, providing information, correcting misconceptions, and providing additional information from comments on these verses in this *Teaching Guide.*

## Encourage Application

7. Lead the class to focus on Jesus' statement in John 12:32. Refer to the *Study Guide* and to this *Teaching Guide* for information, including: John's use of the term "exalted"; the possible double meaning; and the connection with the Greeks (12:20). Challenge the class to answer this question: *What is the significance of Jesus offering himself to draw ALL people to him?*

8. To encourage application ask the class to form groups of three and share their response to the following question: *What has been the significance in your life of Jesus' having offered himself to draw YOU to him?* Allow sufficient time for the class members to share; then close in a prayer of thanksgiving.

## Teaching Plan—Lecture and Questions

### Connect with Life

1.  After welcoming the class and opening with prayer, lead the class in one of the following activities: (1) Use the "Riddles" exercise described in step 1 of "Teaching Plan—Varied Learning Activities"; or (2) Engage the class in a discussion by starting with the question, *What are some things that people are drawn to?* After the class members share their responses, ask, *What are some things that you are drawn to?* Explain that in today's text the Gospel of John shows Jesus' understanding of his mission and demonstrates Jesus' clear intent to follow God's will for his life—to offer himself so as to draw all people to himself.

### Guide Bible Study

2.  Use the following outline to lead the class to explore the focal text. Base your comments on the information in the *Study Guide* and in "Bible Comments" in this *Teaching Guide*. Provide a balance in your presentation between sharing information and providing for discussion. To help your class members stay focused, post the outline on the board or on a poster, or distribute it as a handout.

    First, overview the thrust of the passage: Nearing the end of his ministry, Jesus shared publicly that he was offering himself so that all could receive eternal life.

    I.  The Leaders Plot to Arrest Jesus (11:55–57)

    *Comments:* This passage provides the backdrop for the drama that follows. Highlight the following: (1) the Pharisees' plan to arrest Jesus; (2) the significance of the Passover time; (3) the significance of the temple setting.
    *Questions:*
    *   Who are the key players in this episode?
    *   What is the dramatic tone of the passage?
    *   Why were the Jewish leaders so threatened by Jesus' presence? Can Jesus' presence be a threat to us today? Why or why not?

    II.  The Greeks Ask to See Jesus (12:20–26)

*Comments:* Highlight (1) the symbolic coming of the Greeks to Jesus; (2) the connection between the coming of the Greeks and Jesus' statement that his "hour has come"; (3) the metaphor of the wheat; and (4) Jesus' statement about those who wish to follow him (12:25).

*Questions:*
- Whom do the Greeks represent?
- Did Jesus have to wait until the coming of the Greeks before moving ahead with his ministry?
- How does John indicate that God is in control of the progress of events?
- What do you think Jesus meant when he said (12:25, NRSV), "Those who love their life lose it, and those who hate their life in this world will keep it for eternal life"? How would you explain that verse to a teenager?

III.  Jesus Commits Himself to His Death (12:27–37)

*Comments:* Highlight the following: (1) the background and significance of the voice from heaven; (2) John's use of double meaning in the term "lifted up"; (3) Jesus' use of the misunderstanding in 12:34; (4) the fulfillment of John 1:11 in 12:37.

*Questions:*
- Why do you think the Father responded audibly to Jesus' prayer?
- How can such a repulsive sight as a crucifixion "draw" people to Jesus?
- Jesus said that in his death he would "draw all" people to him. Does this mean that all will be saved? Why or why not?
- Why do you think Jesus hid himself? Does Jesus still hide himself today?

IV.  Jesus Appeals to the People One Final Time (12:44–50)

*Comments:* Highlight the following: (1) the summary of Jesus' message and ministry in these verses; (2) the use of the motif of light and darkness; (3) Jesus' relationship with the Father; (4) the ultimatum of belief.

*Questions:*
- Do you find Jesus' words harsh? Why or why not?
- How do you understand Jesus' statements about himself and the Father?

- What do you think Jesus meant when he said that his "words" would judge?

## Encourage Application

3.  Distribute paper and pencils to the class. Ask members to list the two people with whom they have the closest relationship. Then ask them to add to the list the name of a close friend, followed by the name of an acquaintance or associate. Encourage them to look at the names on their lists and to answer prayerfully these questions to themselves (ask one question at a time and pause to allow the class to work through their response): *Has this person responded to Jesus' call to eternal life? How is God calling me to respond to this person?*

    Next, have them add one more name to the list—their own. Invite them to answer silently the following questions: *How have you been drawn to Jesus' sacrifice for you? How have you responded to Jesus' call to eternal life? How is God calling you to respond today to his being "raised up"?*

4.  Allow sufficient time for the students to respond privately and prayerfully to these questions. Then close in a prayer of thanksgiving for Jesus' sacrifice.

## Focal Text

John 13:1–17

## Background

John 13:1–30

## Main Idea

As Jesus approached his death, he provided us an example of humble service that is to characterize the lives of Christians, too.

## Question to Explore

When do you do as Jesus did in washing the disciples' feet?

## Teaching Aim

To lead the class to identify ways they will follow Jesus' example of service

## UNIT FOUR

*Jesus' Glorious Triumph*

## Lesson Ten

# Do As Jesus Did

## BIBLE COMMENTS

### Understanding the Context

The focal text (13:1–17) centers on Jesus washing the disciples' feet and its significance.

In the remainder of the background text (13:18–30), Jesus moved quickly from his teaching on humility to a prediction of his betrayal by one of the disciples. At least eleven of them were shocked and saddened by his revelation. He had said earlier, "Have I not chosen you, the Twelve? Yet one of you is a devil" (John 6:70). In 13:18, Jesus repeated the cry of Psalm 41:9 about being betrayed by a friend with whom the psalmist had shared bread.

Jesus' purpose in predicting his betrayal was twofold. First, it prepared the disciples to believe in him further as the promised Messiah. He said, "I am telling you now before it happens, so that when it does happen you will believe that I am He" (13:19). He then repeated the often-used statement about his relationship to the Father (13:20).

Jesus had given a vague notice that one of the Twelve was not "clean" (13:10b), but they were still unsuspecting. His heart was heavy as he then clearly told them that "one of you is going to betray me" (13:21). Peter then motioned to "the disciple whom Jesus loved," who was on the

111

right side of Jesus, to ask which one it was (13:23–24). Jesus said it was the one to whom he would give a piece of bread (13:26). When Judas took the bread, he gave way completely to Satanic power. Jesus instructed him to leave quickly (13:27). Even the disciples did not understand that Judas was the betrayer. They assumed he, being the treasurer, had gone to purchase food for the poor.

The second purpose of Jesus' revelation of his coming betrayal (13:18) was for Judas' benefit. We must not overlook the many ways Jesus sought to save Judas from this tragic action. Judas still had the power of choice. First, Jesus washed Judas's feet. By so doing, Jesus showed to him "the full extent of his love" (13:1). Second, Jesus gave Judas the piece of bread he had dipped in the dish (13:26). For a host to do this was a sign of honor and friendship. Third, for Jesus so easily to hand Judas the bread, Judas must have been seated on his left, a place of honor. Fourth, even the statement, "What you are about to do, do quickly" (13:27), gave Judas a last chance to repent of his intended betrayal. It was decision time for Judas. He made the wrong decision. He "went out. And it was night" (13:30).

## Interpreting the Scriptures

The synoptic gospels tell of Jesus' instructions for the preparation of the Passover meal (Matthew 26:17–19; Mark 14:12–16; Luke 22:7–12). They also include the institution of the Lord's Supper. John includes neither but rather emphasizes the depth of divine love manifested at this last meal with Jesus' disciples before his death.

### Love Stoops to Serve (13:1–5)

**13:1.** John's phrase "just before the Passover Feast" likely means just before the beginning of the meal. It was on Thursday evening, one day before Jesus' trial and crucifixion. As they met in the upper room, Jesus knew that the final act of redemption was at hand. Jesus had said in John 12:23, "The hour has come for the Son of Man to be glorified." This statement referred to his impending death, followed by his resurrection and return to his Father. It was the hour for which Jesus was born, the hour of both his humiliation and glorification. It was the hour of judgment on the world and victory over Satan.

"Having loved his own" is a direct reference to those faithful disciples who had given much and endured much to follow him and who would face even greater trials in the future. Jesus' expression of love for these followers does not indicate a lesser love for all followers, then and now, however.

**13:2.** The Gospel of John states that, prior to the Passover meal, Satan had already tempted Judas to betray Jesus. The synoptic gospels report that earlier in the week Judas had conspired with the chief priests to deliver Jesus into their hands (Matt. 26:14–16; Mark 14:10–11; Luke 22:3–6).

**13:3–5.** Jesus had come from God, had been given dominion over all things, and knew he was soon to return to the Father. Even so he "made himself nothing, taking the very nature of a servant" (Philippians 2:7). Much to the astonishment of the disciples, Jesus arose from the table and prepared to wash their feet.

Foot-washing was not just a ritual in Palestine; it was a practical necessity. The roads were unpaved and therefore dusty in dry weather and muddy in wet weather. The sandals they wore did little to protect their feet from dust or mud. A servant would wash the feet of those who entered. Having no servants, the disciples probably took turns at this task. In this instance, however, no disciple volunteered to assume this responsibility. Why? Luke 22:24 states that "a dispute arose among them as to which of them was considered to be greatest." With such an attitude, they were unwilling to wash the feet of another disciple. Thus, Jesus arose and began to wash their feet.

There are always some people in churches who are unwilling to do the menial tasks or serve in the more obscure ministries. When we are tempted to pride, we should think of our Savior on his knees, washing the feet of the disciples. A task that did not threaten Jesus' dignity should not threaten ours.

## The Reluctance of the Disciples (13:6–14)

**13:6–7.** As Jesus continued to wash the disciples' feet, at last he came to Peter. All the disciples were likely embarrassed by Jesus' action, but they remained silent. It was left to Peter—who, like many people, approached every situation with an open mouth—to question Christ's humble service. "Lord, are you going to wash my feet" (13:6b) seems more of a statement of disbelief than a question. Jesus said that although Peter did not understand the significance of what he was doing, "later you will understand" (13:7). Christ could have meant his explanation in 13:12–17, but more than likely he meant after the resurrection and the coming of the Holy Spirit who "will teach you all things and will remind you of everything I have said to you" (John 14:26).

**13:8–9.** Peter became more adamant when he declared that Jesus would never wash his feet. Christ's response indicated a far deeper meaning than simply washing the dust from Peter's feet. Such submission to Christ was necessary for continued companionship and fellowship. When Peter learned what was to be lost, he went overboard. He asked Jesus to wash not only his feet but also his hands and his head.

**13:10–11.** Jesus' answer to Peter had a physical context as well as a spiritual meaning. It was customary for people going to a feast to bathe before leaving home. Upon arrival at the feast, only their feet needed washing. The disciples presumably had bathed prior to the Passover Feast.

The spiritual meaning had to do with the disciples' conversion experience, their new birth. Titus 3:5 refers to Christ's having "saved us through the washing of rebirth." However, even Christians continue to commit sin from time to time, which affects our fellowship with God, and from which we need forgiveness.

Jesus referred to Judas when he told Peter, "You are clean, though not every one of you" (John 13:10).

## The Application of the Lesson (13:12–17)

**13:12.** When Jesus had completed washing the disciples' feet, he took his place at the table again. He asked them whether they understood what he had done for them. He did not wait for an answer.

**13:13–15.** Jesus told the disciples that since they called him "'Teacher' and 'Lord'" then they ought to heed his instructions and follow his example. If One held in such high esteem would stoop to wash another's feet, then the disciples ought to be willing to do the same.

There is no scriptural evidence that Jesus intended foot-washing to become a Christian ordinance. Paul's writings mention baptism and the Lord's Supper, but not foot-washing. Jesus taught that these two ordinances were to be observed to the end of the age. He instructed us to "go and make disciples of all nations, baptizing them . . . And surely I am with you always, to the very end of the age" (Matt. 28:20). In speaking of the Lord's Supper, Jesus said, "Do this in remembrance of me" (Luke 22:19). Paul said that when we observe the Lord's Supper, we "proclaim the Lord's death until he comes" (1 Corinthians 11:26). No such exalted statements are made concerning foot-washing.

**13:16–17.** We often hear the phrase, "Like father, like son." Jesus taught, *Like master, like servant.* Since Jesus, their Master, was not too proud to do menial service, then the disciples ought to humble themselves to do likewise. The same applies to us today. As his followers, we are subordinate to him, and from him we receive our authority to serve.

The emphasis of verse 17 is on doing as well as hearing and understanding. Jesus said (Luke 6:46), "Why do you call me 'Lord, Lord,' and do not do what I say?" We must do the will of our heavenly Father (see Matt. 7:21). At the conclusion of the Sermon on the Mount, Jesus said, "Therefore everyone who hears these words of mine and puts them into practice is like a wise man" (Matt. 7:24). True blessings come not simply from understanding the meaning of what we have received from Christ, but also from following his example in humble service.

## Focusing on the Meaning

The lesson today focuses on these matters: forgiveness, not verbally expressed but manifested by an act of kindness; humility, being willing to assume the role of a servant; and service, portrayed by Jesus performing a needed service, a menial task.

An example of forgiveness: Jesus was betrayed by Judas; however, there is no evidence of bitterness but every evidence by Jesus' actions of a willingness to forgive. An opposite attitude was assumed by a pastor who was betrayed by a church member whom he had befriended in many ways. The man joined with two strong leaders in the church to call for the pastor's resignation. Although the pastor moved to another church and continued his ministry until his retirement, there was always bitterness in his heart toward these men. We must follow Jesus' example when from the cross he looked at those responsible for putting him there and prayed, "Father, forgive them" (Luke 23:34). Bitterness erodes emotional and spiritual health; forgiveness enhances both.

An example of humility: On Maundy Thursday evening in our church a pastor from a neighboring church shared his personal testimony. He related a meeting with five deacons who informed him that they had lost confidence in his pastoral leadership. They asked him to take two weeks to determine what his response would be. He spent much time in prayer, meditation, and reading the Bible. It was while reading John 13 that he began to feel God leading him to wash the deacons' feet. When he met again with these deacons, he told them he would give them his decision after he did what God has impressed him to do. He took a towel, knelt before the deacon chairman, wiped his shoes, asked his forgiveness, and prayed for him through his tears. The deacon arose and proceeded to wipe the shoes of the pastor and also prayed for him. Reconciliation had taken place. The experience, the pastor explained, had given him a better understanding of what Jesus meant when he washed the disciples feet—that God uses those who humble themselves.

An example of humble service: A pastor of a small church was visiting in the home of an elderly widower, a man with whom he had a close relationship. While there the pastor noticed the man's bare feet. The man's toenails need trimming. With the man's permission, the pastor knelt and performed this service.

A second example of humble service: One of the ways our church follows Jesus' example is through our "Heart Ministry." In addition to phone calls and cards, volunteers visit the homebound, those in hospitals and nursing homes, those in grief, and those experiencing emergencies and special needs. For example, one family had premature triplets. After months in the hospital, they were sent home. Volunteers came to the home once or twice a week to assist with mixing formula, changing diapers, feeding the babies, and giving them a little extra attention and cuddling. All of this was done in the name of Jesus, who humbled himself, took up a towel, and began to wash the disciples' feet.

# TEACHING PLANS

## Teaching Plan—Varied Learning Activities

### Connect with Life

1. Before class begins move all the chairs to one corner of the room. Write the following question on the board: *When I think of great service at a restaurant, I think of . . . .* As each person enters the room,

escort him or her to the spot in the room where they would prefer to sit and ask the person to wait one moment. Then bring a chair to them and invite them to have a seat. Inquire whether there is anything else you could do for them, such as bring them coffee, a book, or a Bible. Ask them to complete the sentence that is on the board. You may wish to enlist other members beforehand to assist you. You could simply ask people to complete the sentence on the board.

## Guide Bible Study

2. State that today's lesson will focus on understanding and applying the example of humble service seen in Jesus as he washed his disciples' feet. Enlist a volunteer to write on the board. Ask the class to share their ideas to complete the sentence that is on the board. Instruct the recorder to write responses on the board as people share. Remember to affirm all answers as they are given. Then read John 13:1–17 aloud and call for someone to lead in prayer.

3. Distribute an 8½" x 11" sheet of paper to each person. Instruct the class to draw a horizontal line across the length of the paper and a vertical line down the middle of the paper, creating four equal squares. Tell them to write one of the following headings at the top of each square, as given in the *Study Guide*:
   • A Portrait of Heritage and Horizon
   • A Portrait of Hospitality and Honor
   • A Portrait of Humility and Humiliation
   • A Portrait of Honesty and Happiness

4. Tell the class that this paper will serve as a picture to guide the study. Remind them that today begins a set of four lessons under the theme, "Jesus' Glorious Triumph." In the square for "Heritage and Horizon," instruct each person to draw or describe a time when he or she had to leave a person they loved, whether for a long or short time, explaining some of the emotions they felt. Summarize the thoughts in the *Study Guide* related to John 13:1. Emphasize that Jesus knew he was about to leave the disciples whom he loved and that his love compelled him to leave them with a very important truth.

5. Using the *Study Guide* comments on John 13:2–5, describe to the class or actually show the class, using a pre-enlisted volunteer, the

act of washing feet. Explain the importance of Jesus being willing to do this act of service because he wanted to and not because he had to. Encourage each person to write under the heading "Hospitality and Honor" three words they would have felt if they had been the first disciple whose feet Jesus washed.

6. Divide the class into two groups. (Form additional groups with duplicate assignments to have groups six people or fewer in size.)

   Ask one group to discuss Peter's response to Jesus, using these questions:
   - Why did Peter respond as he did in verse 6?
   - Why did he continue to resist in verse 8?
   - Why did he respond as he did in verse 9?
   - What application to life today does this encounter suggest to you?

   Ask the other group to discuss Jesus' response to Peter, using these questions:
   - Why did Jesus wash the disciples' feet?
   - Why do you think Jesus insisted on washing Peter's feet after he protested?
   - What application to life today does this encounter suggest to you?

   Encourage each group to review the *Study Guide* section on John 13:6–11 as well as add their thoughts. After a few minutes, call on each group for a brief report. Invite each person to jot down truths that come to mind while listening to the reports. They can write these truths in the square under the heading, "Humility and Humiliation."

7. Explain John 13:12–17 by using information from the *Study Guide* and from this *Teaching Guide*. Remind the people that Jesus wanted the disciples to understand why he did what he did. Ask each person to write under the heading, "Honesty and Happiness," a one-sentence response to Jesus' question in John 13:12, "Do you understand what I have done for you?"

## Encourage Application

UNIT FOUR: Jesus' Glorious Triumph

8. Invite the class to read the small article related to R.C. Buckner. Then ask, *What are some things we can do to follow Jesus' example of serving others?* Close the lesson by reading aloud John 13:17.

## Teaching Plan—Lecture and Questions

### Connect with Life

1. Prior to class, fill four small cups with water and place them on a table beside an empty pitcher. Write on the board the Main Idea of today's lesson as stated in the *Study Guide*.

2. Describe one personal experience of good service at a restaurant and one bad. Read the Main Idea from the board and state that today we will look to Jesus to discover the most authentic way to serve others. Read John 13:1–17 aloud.

### Guide Bible Study

3. Summarize the *Study Guide* comments on John 13:1–5, stressing the fact that Jesus was doing an act of service and kindness to those he loved because he wanted to and not because he had to. Remind the people that this was one of the last times he saw the disciples. Ask the class what significance the phrase in 13:1, "the time had come," would have on the behavior of Jesus. Ask, *What mood or attitude do you think Jesus might have been in?*

4. Invite the class to follow as you read the small article in the *Study Guide* related to R.C. Buckner. Read John 13:5 aloud again. Pour one of the cups of water into the pitcher. Then refer to question 4 in the *Study Guide*, and ask, *What are some qualities of a servant leader?*

5. Read John 13:6–11 aloud to the class. Using the *Study Guide*, describe to the class some possible reasons Peter responded the way he did in the conversation with Jesus. Ask the class to add other possible thoughts Peter must have been having. Invite someone to offer a prayer of thanksgiving to God for the security believers have in Christ Jesus. Remind them that once a person has been saved there may be times of renewal and refreshing needed in our lives,

but we can never lose our salvation. Pour the second cup of water into the pitcher.

6. Ask the class to read silently John 13:12–17. As they read, pour the third cup of water into the pitcher. Using the *Study Guide* notes, explain to the class the unique lesson Jesus wanted his disciples to learn.

## Encourage Application

7. Refer the class to the small article in the *Study Guide* related to the "Divine Servant." After the class has read it, lead them to add answers to the question in the article, *How can we become servant leaders?*

8. Read John 13:12 again to the class. Explain that the true test of whether we understand what Jesus did will be found in our response to verse 17. Emphasize that Jesus said we would be happy if we put his teachings into practice. Pour the fourth cup of water into the pitcher.

9. Comment that today we have seen in the life of Jesus an example of humble service. Like the pitcher, we have been filled with his word. Now, as we leave, let all of us commit to pouring this knowledge into the lives of people we meet this week by "washing their feet" with actions of love.

## Focal Text

John 14:15–27; 15:26—16:15

## Background

John 13:31—17:26

## Main Idea

Jesus continues to provide encouragement and strength for Christian living to all who turn to him.

## Question to Explore

How can you face challenges to and concerns about your faith?

## Teaching Aim

To lead the class to describe implications for their lives of the sources of encouragement and strength for Christian living identified in these Scriptures

## UNIT FOUR

### Jesus' Glorious Triumph

# Lesson Eleven

# Never Alone

## BIBLE COMMENTS

### Understanding the Context

The focal text concentrates on the promise of the Holy Spirit and the Spirit's standing alongside the believer to give help for Christian living and service. The background text deals with additional themes.

Glorification is one theme that is prominent in the background text. John 13:31–32 refers to Jesus' glorification through his death and resurrection, in which both the Father and the Son are glorified. Jesus' response to prayers offered in his name brings glory to the Father (14:13). Abiding in Christ, the vine, and bearing much fruit brings glory to God (15:8). In 17:1–5 Jesus prayed for himself. He acknowledged that he had glorified the Father by obediently completing the work assigned to him. Jesus then asked that God glorify him by restoring him to the glory he had with the Father prior to his incarnation.

Another theme, the theme of Jesus' "going away," prompted numerous questions. In 13:33 Jesus told his disciples, "I will be with you only a little longer." Peter asked Jesus where he was going and why he could not follow him now. Jesus replied that Peter could follow him later. Jesus then told Peter he would deny him three times (see 13:36–38). In 14:1–5 Jesus told his disciples he was going to prepare a place for them. Thomas said that he did not know where Jesus was going and asked, "How can we know the way?" (14:5). Jesus replied, "I am the way, the truth, and the life" (14:6). In 14:8–9 Jesus responded to Philip's statement by asking, "How can you say, 'Show us the Father'?" Jesus stated that anyone who had seen him had also seen the Father (14:7–9). In 14:28 Jesus prepared the disciples for his going away. In 16:17 some of Jesus' disciples asked, "What does he mean by saying 'In a little while you will see me no more, and then after a little while you will see me'?" Jesus replied that they would grieve when he left but would rejoice when he returned (16:22).

Jesus' discussion of the vine and the branches, a third theme in the background text, is recorded in 15:1–8. There are three characters: Jesus, the vine; the Father, the gardener; and Christ's followers, the branches. There are three functions: Jesus, the Source of life; the Father, who does the pruning; and the followers, who produce the fruit. The unfruitful branches are pruned in order for the healthy branches to produce much fruit. The unfruitful branches may represent those who have only an intellectual belief in Christ but are not committed heart, mind, and soul. Just as the branch must be in continual contact with the vine, the followers of Christ must maintain a vital union with him. The threefold blessing that issues out of our abiding in Christ is that we bear fruit, we find our prayers are answered, and we glorify the Father (15:5–8).

## Interpreting the Scriptures

### A Helper Is Promised to Those Who Love (14:15–17)

Love is one of the major themes of Jesus. He said that we are to love one another as he has loved us. By this love, others will know we are Jesus' followers (13:34–35). Christ's love for us is in direct relation to the Father's love for him. We remain in Christ's love as we live in obedience to his command (15:9–10). We, therefore, should not be surprised that receiving the Holy Spirit is dependent on our love for Jesus and our obedience to his commands.

Jesus said he would petition the Father, who would give us "another Counselor" (14:16). The Greek word translated "Counselor" is *Paraclete*, which means *one who is called alongside to provide help, guidance, and defense.* In this context, the words "Comforter" (KJV), "Helper" (NASB), and "Advocate" (NRSV) are also appropriate.

The *Paraclete* is referred to as *another Paraclete*, which suggests that Jesus was also a Paraclete, a Helper. The Spirit's ministry is to resemble Christ's in many ways.

During his earthly ministry, Jesus was with his followers for a short period of time. The Holy Spirit will be with them forever.

The "world"—those who live apart from God—cannot receive the Spirit because they have rejected the revelation of God in Jesus Christ (14:17). The word "knows" (14:17) refers to experiential knowledge that the unbeliever does not have. However, the believers know him, for the Spirit dwells within them, representing the Christ in whom they have believed.

## The Promised Reappearance (14:18–24)

**14:18–20.** These verses can be interpreted in two ways. One interpretation is that the reference continues to be a promise of the Holy Spirit: "I will not leave you as orphans"—that is, fatherless or comfortless (14:18). Jesus would be present with the disciples in a more profound manner through the indwelling of the Holy Spirit. Thus, they never would need to feel lonely as an orphan. Another interpretation is that these verses are a reference to Jesus' resurrection appearances. Jesus said he would come to the disciples and they would see him. John 16:16 may reinforce this view.

Both interpretations might be correct. Jesus might have had a twofold meaning in mind. Regardless, the effect of either event would result in the disciples' recognition of Jesus' relationship to the Father and their relationship to him.

**14:21.** Jesus returned to the theme of obedience to his commands as a manifestation of one's love, which, in turn, guarantees the love of the Father.

**14:22–24.** Judas (not Iscariot) asked why Jesus was going to manifest himself to the disciples and not to the world. This disciple likely was still thinking in terms of an earthly kingdom in which the Messiah would manifest himself to the world. He interpreted Jesus' remarks as a change of plans. Jesus replied that those who do not love him and are not obedient to him will not be capable of receiving his manifestation. For those who love Jesus, both he and the Father would make their abode with them through the indwelling presence of the Holy Spirit.

## The Holy Spirit As Teacher (14:25–27)

**14:25.** "All this I have spoken" refers not only to the truth Jesus shared in the upper room, but also to all the truth he had revealed to them from the beginning of his ministry.

**14:26–27.** The need for the Holy Spirit, both for the disciples and for us, is that we do not remember all that Jesus taught. Even if we remember, we do not understand the full meaning. The Holy Spirit has come not to bring a new revelation but to remind us of the things Jesus taught and to interpret their meaning. For example, the disciples did not understand the full significance of Jesus' triumphant entry into Jerusalem until after the resurrection (John 12:16). Jesus further reminded the disciples that peace would be part of the legacy he was leaving them as he went away and sent the Spirit (14:27).

## A Twofold Witness (15:26–27)

Jesus underscored the fact that the Holy Spirit would be sent from the Father and that the Spirit is "the Spirit of truth" (15:26). The Spirit's ministry is also one of bearing witness to all that Jesus taught and did. The Spirit's witness is not to be apart from the ministry of the disciples. It is through them that the Spirit works to declare the truth of God. These disciples were well-qualified because they had been with Jesus from the beginning of Jesus' ministry. Still, they would need the enlightenment of the Spirit to be effective witnesses. Jesus said, "You will receive power when the Holy Spirit comes on you and you will be my witnesses . . ." (Acts 1:8).

It is significant that the command to be witnesses came following Jesus' declaration that because of their relationship to him, they, too, would suffer hatred and persecution (15:18–21). The reassurance of Matthew 10:19–20 would be helpful. It was a promise that when the time of testing came, they would be given what to say, for the Holy Spirit would be speaking through them.

## A Warning Concerning Persecution (16:1–4)

**16:1–2.** "All this" refers to what Jesus had told them previously (15:18–27). He warned the disciples of inevitable persecution so that when it came they would not forsake the faith. Jesus described the persecution in terms of death itself as well as their being denied access to the synagogue. These executions would be by those who believed they were doing God a favor by killing the heretics. Saul (Paul) is a good example of this belief (Philippians 3:6), and Stephen is an example of those slain (Acts 7:54–60).

**16:3–4.** Having known neither Jesus nor the Father, the Jewish leaders persecuted the believers. There was no excuse for their ignorance, for Jesus had given them ample opportunity to believe in him as the promised Messiah.

While Jesus was with the disciples, he was a shield between his enemies and the disciples. When Jesus was gone, the disciples would be the objects of persecution.

## The Ministry of the Holy Spirit (16:5–11).

**16:5–7.** Even though Jesus declared that he was returning to the Father who sent him, the disciples did not ask (16:5), "Where are you going?" The fact that Jesus was leaving obscured any concern as to where he was going. Their selfish concern for themselves outweighed any happiness that Jesus was returning to his former glory. It may be that, even in the shadow of the cross, the disciples were still hoping for an earthly kingdom. Christ's leaving would dash those hopes.

Jesus explained that it would be to their advantage for him to go away. At this point the disciples were blind to any advantage they would gain through loss. While in bodily form, Jesus was limited by time and place. The Holy Spirit has no such limitation. The Spirit would fulfill Jesus' promise that he would be with them "always, to the very end of the age" (Matt. 28:20). Inasmuch as the Spirit's ministry was to interpret the completed ministry of Jesus, that could not be done until after Jesus' crucifixion, resurrection, and ascension.

**16:8–11.** The work of the Holy Spirit as prosecutor is set forth in these verses. The three words used—"sin," "righteousness," and "judgment"—are defining factors in one's spiritual state. Sin here is described as unbelief. The Holy Spirit will convict the non-believing world that failing to believe in Christ constitutes the world's greatest sin.

Those who crucified Christ sought to put him to shame. Jesus' resurrection and return to the Father removed the shame and validated his righteousness. The sinful world stands condemned by the righteousness of Christ.

The Holy Spirit is the advocate for the believer and the prosecutor for the unbeliever. The Spirit brings judgment because of one's relationship to the "prince of this world" (16:11). This judgment began when Christ was lifted up on the cross and Satan's defeat was predicted.

### The Spirit Reveals the Truth of Christ (16:12–15)

**16:12–13.** A person can assimilate knowledge only according to his or her ability to understand. This was the case of the disciples at the time of Jesus' departure. It would become the ministry of the Holy Spirit to enlarge their understanding of the teachings of Jesus' life, death, and resurrection. Just as Jesus received what he taught from the Father, the Holy Spirit would interpret to Jesus' followers what Jesus taught. The truth that the Holy Spirit was to teach was not to be additional truth, but truth reflected in Jesus.

Whatever the phrase "he will tell you what is yet to come" means, it does not mean a new revelation such as that claimed by Mary Baker Eddy, founder of Christian Science, or by Joseph Smith, founder of Latter Day Saints. It could mean that the Holy Spirit would enable the disciples to understand more fully the predictions of Jesus, such as those in Mark 13:1–37. It could refer as well to such predictions as those recorded in 1 Thessalonians 4:13–18; 5:1–3, or those in the Revelation.

**16:14–15.** Just as Jesus glorified the Father by his obedience, his teaching, and his atoning death, so also the Holy Spirit would glorify the Son by interpreting the meaning of Christ's teachings and ministry. "What is mine" refers to the message that the Father had given Jesus (16:15). This is the message the Holy Spirit will make known to us.

### The Lord's Prayer (17:1–26)

**17:1–5.** All of John 17 is indeed "the Lord's prayer." It is divided into three different petitions. In verses 1–5 Jesus prayed for himself. (See "Understanding the Context.")

**17:6–19.** The second petition is for Jesus' disciples. Jesus did not pray for the disciples to be removed from the world but that they be protected while in the world by the power and character of God's name. Just as Jesus was their guardian while on earth, now they were to be under the protective care of the Father. This is another assurance that they were not to be orphans but to have the presence of the Father through the Holy Spirit (17:11–12).

Jesus concluded his prayer for his disciples by returning to his desire that they might experience the fullness of joy (17:13; see also 15:11). He also prayed that they might be sanctified; that is, set apart for the task assigned them (17:17).

**17:20–26.** Jesus then prayed for all believers who would receive the message of the disciples. It was a prayer for spiritual unity based on a common life for, and faith in, Jesus Christ. The result of this unity was to be a testimony to the world of the validity of Christ, who was sent from God.

## Focusing on the Meaning

*Promise fulfilled.* The fulfillment of the promise of the Holy Spirit came on the day of Pentecost while the followers of Jesus met in the upper room. They were empowered to witness as never before.

*Fruit of the Spirit.* Galatians 5:22 lists the fruit of the Spirit. "Fruit" is singular in that verse, indicating that each Christian is to possess all nine characteristics of a Spirit-filled life, not just one or two favorites.

*Witness.* The command to be a witness is not optional (John 15:27; Acts 1:8). If Jonas Salk had withheld his vaccine for polio, thousands would have died from the disease. Inasmuch as we are able to share the truth that saves, it is criminal to withhold our witness from the unbelieving world.

*Guidance for us.* The object lesson God gave Elijah in 1 Kings 19:10–12 can serve as an example of how God works today through the "still, small voice." God can speak to us through the dramatic experiences of life, but more often it is in the quietness of our souls that the Holy Spirit gives us guidance and a sense of God's presence.

*Jesus the criterion by which to interpret the Bible.* Jesus said that what he taught was directly from the Father and that the Holy Spirit's ministry was to interpret what Jesus said and did. This truth indicates that Jesus is indeed the criterion by which the Bible is to be interpreted.

*Facets of the Spirit's ministry.* John gives us different facets of the ministry of the Holy Spirit. He is described as Helper or Advocate (14:15–17); Teacher (14:25–26); Witness (15:26–27); Prosecutor (16:8–11); and Revealer (16:12–15).

# TEACHING PLANS

## Teaching Plan—Varied Learning Activities

### Connect with Life

1. Point out that in this lesson, as with the previous lesson, the setting is the last evening of Jesus' earthly life and that Jesus was continuing to prepare his disciples for what was to come. In the previous lesson, Jesus showed the disciples by example how they were to serve one another. Now he shared his final instructions by comforting his disciples, promising the presence of the Holy Spirit, and offering encouragement through prayer.

2. Encourage each person to think of three to five emotions that people might experience when they are totally alone after a time of crisis. After about one minute, enlist a volunteer to write on the board. Encourage everyone to call out an emotion. Repeat this until many emotions are listed. State that Jesus knew that his disciples were about to experience many different emotions as well as a sense of loneliness. Therefore, in some of his final remarks, he reminded them that they would never be alone.

### Guide Bible Study

3. Divide the class into three groups. Explain to the class that each group is going to write a brief survival guide for Christians. Tell them they are to identify five to seven survival guide tips. Each tip can be no longer than two sentences. Instruct them to use only the Scripture assigned to them. Each group will need one person to serve as a recorder. Distribute paper and ask each recorder to write across the top of the page, "Survival Guide for Christians." Assign one of the following to each group:
   • John 14
   • John 15
   • John 16

To assist them in their work, write on the board the following questions and share with the class they may use the questions to help them complete their work if needed.

- How can a Christian find strength to face difficult times?
- How do Christians encourage one another?
- What are some of the roles or functions of the Holy Spirit?
- How can a Christian have peace and fulfillment?

Encourage the groups to be both creative and realistic. Allow fifteen-to-twenty minutes for this activity. Then invite one person from each group to read their survival guide tips to the entire class.

## Encourage Application

4. Read John 14:26–27 aloud. Remind the class that Jesus promised his followers that they would never be alone. Encourage the people to "tap into" the resource of the Holy Spirit that resides in them. Emphasize that the survival guide tips they have discovered in today's lesson are available to each of them. Ask for one or two volunteers to share how they plan to use one of the tips in the coming week. Then ask someone to pray for the ones who shared.

5. Prior to class, enlist a minister or counselor to prepare a five-minute presentation on the effects of loneliness. Also, encourage the person to share, in their opinion, ways someone can help a person deal with loneliness.

6. Summarize the comments in this *Teaching Guide* on John 17, especially that it records Jesus' prayer for himself, his disciples, and all believers. Encourage each person to read John 17 sometime before they go to sleep tonight. Challenge the class to understand that just as Jesus prayed, we too must pray in order to receive the strength needed for our lives.

7. Close the lesson by letting the three groups (see step 3) have a time of prayer for one another. Encourage them to be specific as they pray. Suggest they call someone in their group during the week and pray for them over the phone.

## Teaching Plan—Lecture and Questions

### Connect with Life

1. Write on the board the Main Idea for today's lesson as found in the *Study Guide.*

2. Prior to class, identify several stories in your local newspaper that are examples of people in need. The need may be social, emotional, physical, or spiritual. Read portions of these articles to the class. Read to the class the Main Idea from the board and lead in prayer.

### Guide Bible Study

3. Under the main idea, write the following key words: *Challenge, Comfort, Counsel, Communication, Change.* Explain to the class that these key words are from the *Study Guide* outline of this lesson and that you will use these key words to guide your comments today. Encourage the class to keep their *Study Guides* open and to feel free to ask questions.

4. Using the *Study Guide* comments related to John 13:31–38, explain to the class that Jesus was still preparing his disciples for the challenges they were to face. Remind the class of last week's lesson where Jesus taught by example the importance of serving one another. Point out the significance of John 13:34. Instruct the class to allow service and love to guide them in facing the challenges of today's world. Circle the word *Challenge* on the board.

5. Share with the class a personal experience in which you needed comfort. Then enlist someone to read aloud John 14:15–27. Using the comments in the *Study Guide* and this *Teaching Guide* related to John 14:15–27, identify and explain the first two roles of the Holy Spirit: Helper and Teacher. Directly apply these two roles by giving an example of how the Spirit brings comfort. You may wish to enlist a person before class to give a brief testimony on how he or she was comforted through a tough time recently. Circle the word *Comfort.*

6. Read John 15:26—16:15 to the class. Circle the word *Counsel* on the board. Using the *Study Guide* comments, identify and explain the third, fourth, and fifth roles of the Holy Spirit (Witness, Prosecutor,

Revealer). Refer the class to the article, "The Youth-Led Revival Movement." Remind them that without the Holy Spirit, no one would be convicted of sin and thus no one would seek Jesus! Review the roles of the Holy Spirit mentioned in John 14—16 (Helper, Teacher, Witness, Prosecutor, Revealer; see "Focusing on the Meaning" in this *Teaching Guide*). Invite the class to share which role of the Holy Spirit they identify with most and why.

7. Circle the words *Communication* and *Change* on the board. Ask the class to turn to John 17 in their Bibles. Tell the class that change comes through prayer! If possible, share with the class a personal experience of how prayer changed your perspective on some event in your life. Using the comments in the *Study Guide* and in this *Teaching Guide* on John 17, summarize Jesus' prayer under the following headings:
   - Jesus Prays for Himself
   - Jesus Prays for His Disciples
   - Jesus Prays for All Believers

## Encourage Application

8. Lead the class to answer the questions in the *Study Guide*.

9. Invite prayer requests concerning challenges to be faced this next week. Lead in prayer.

## Focal Text

John 19:1–21, 26–30

## Background

John 18—19

## Main Idea

Jesus willingly gave his life to fulfill his mission of drawing all people to himself.

## Question to Explore

What was "finished" at Jesus' crucifixion?

## Teaching Aim

To help the class explain how Jesus' death affects their lives today

**UNIT FOUR**

*Jesus' Glorious Triumph*

## Lesson Twelve

# "It Is Finished"

## BIBLE COMMENTS

### Understanding the Context

In John 18:1–11 Jesus and his disciples left the upper room for the Garden of Gethsemane. There they were encountered by both temple police and Roman soldiers, led by Judas. Jesus took the initiative by asking (18:4), "Who is it you want?" "Jesus of Nazareth" was the reply, to which Jesus said, "I am he" (18:5). Such a powerful statement caused the soldiers to fall back. After the question and answer was repeated, Jesus allowed them to take him away, with the request that his disciples go free. After Peter cut off the ear of Malchus, Jesus rebuked Peter, declaring that he was to drink the cup the Father had given him.

Jesus was taken to Annas, a former high priest and the father-in-law of Caiaphas, the ruling high priest. Although Annas had relinquished his position, he still had power and influence (see 18:12–14, 19–24). Ignoring the accepted procedure of supplying a witness to testify against a prisoner, Annas began immediately to question Jesus about his disciples and his teachings. Jesus suggested that since he had taught in the synagogues as well as in the temple, Annas should get the testimony of those who had heard him. In response to being struck by a soldier, Jesus replied that he had done no wrong, for he had spoken the truth. Jesus was then sent to Caiaphas, the ruling high priest. The Gospel of John gives no statement about the proceedings before Caiaphas.

Peter's denial of Jesus is recorded in 18:15–18, 25–27. Peter had followed Jesus to the courtyard of the high priest. The "other disciple," who had influence, gained Peter's entrance into the courtyard. Here, in response to questions about his relationship with Jesus, Peter denied the accusation three times. The rooster crowed even as Jesus had prophesied.

Following Jesus' encounter with Caiaphas, he was taken at an early hour to the palace of Pilate, the Roman governor (18:28–40). Not wanting to be contaminated and miss the Passover, the Jews would not enter the palace. Pilate accommodated them by meeting them in front of the palace. When Pilate asked about the charges, they replied that Jesus was a criminal. They were forced to reveal their intended purpose—the crucifixion of Jesus—when Pilate told them to try Jesus by their own law. Crucifixion was not in the power of the Jewish court.

When Pilate asked Jesus whether he were king of the Jews and what he had done, Jesus explained that his kingdom was spiritual and not earthly. Pilate perceived that Jesus indeed was some kind of king. Jesus acknowledged that he came into the world to testify to the truth, and that his reign was in the hearts of those who were on the side of truth.

Convinced of Jesus' innocence, Pilate tried to save him by giving the Jews a choice between releasing Jesus or Barabbas. They cried, "Give us Barabbas" (18:40). The focal text picks up with Pilate's continued dealings with Jesus, which ultimately resulted in his crucifixion.

## Interpreting the Scriptures

### Jesus Scourged and Mocked (19:1–3)

**19:1.** Pilate was appointed governor of Judea in 26 AD. He attempted to obscure his weakness by his obstinacy and acts of violence. He had little use for the Jews and offended them often by what he said and did.

Knowing that Jesus had done nothing deserving of death, Pilate attempted again to avoid condemning him. He had Jesus flogged in the hope that this would satisfy the Jews (see Luke 23:15–16). The whip used had pieces of metal or bone attached to it and thus left Jesus' body a bloody pulp. Isaiah had written centuries before, "He was crushed for our iniquities . . . and by his wounds we are healed" (Isaiah 53:5).

**19:2–3.** The soldiers had evidently heard the accusation that Jesus claimed to be king of the Jews. Thus they mocked him by putting a crown made from thorns on his head, a discarded robe on his body, and a staff instead of a scepter in his hand (see Matthew 27:29). They then marched around him, spitting in his face and slapping him while shouting, "Hail, king of the Jews."

### Pilate Again Attempts to Avoid Condemning Jesus (19:4–7)

**19:4–5.** The scourging had taken place inside the palace. Now, hoping that seeing the bleeding body of Jesus would be sufficient to satisfy the Jewish leaders, Pilate brought Jesus outside. Pilate said, "Here is the man!" What man was he? He was the man sent from God, but now a pathetic figure. He was in the process of following the will of the Father to bring salvation to all humankind, even to those calling for his death.

**19:6–7.** The Jews cried, "Crucify!" Their angry cry convinced Pilate that his plan had failed. Declaring again that he found no grounds for condemnation, he told the chief priests to take Jesus and crucify him, knowing they did not have that authority.

The Jewish leaders knew then that the charge of sedition was not going to bring the desired result. They turned then to a new charge—that Jesus claimed to be the Son of God. They relied on Leviticus 24:16 to condemn him: "Anyone who blasphemes the name of the Lord must be put to death." They were not dismissing their charge that Jesus claimed to be king of the Jews, a claim that threatened Roman rule and was thus a capital offence, but rather adding to it the weight of their own religious law. Pilate "was even more afraid," knowing that he must give the situation serious attention (19:8).

### Second Interrogation and Attempted Release of Jesus (19:8–12)

**19:8–9.** The pagans believed that gods could appear in the form of human beings (see Acts 14:11). Upon hearing the Jews charging that Jesus claimed to be the Son of God, Pilate became fearful. He was already in awe of Jesus. This charge only added to his insecurity.

---

UNIT FOUR: Jesus' Glorious Triumph

Pilate returned Jesus to the palace and asked him where he came from. Was he of earth or heaven? Jesus remained silent. Why? One can only speculate. Perhaps Jesus thought he had answered that question already in the first interrogation when he said that his kingdom was not of this world and that he had come into the world to testify of the truth (18:36). Jesus knew no other statement would be understood.

**19:10–11.** Pilate was upset by Jesus' silence, looking on it as an insult to his position. He reminded Jesus that he had the power to release him or condemn him to death. Jesus responded by challenging his power in the light of a greater authority from which Pilate received his authority. Jesus could be referring to general civil authority, as in Romans 13:1, or to the specific power granted to Pilate for the condemnation and crucifixion of Jesus.

The reference to someone committing a greater sin than Pilate may refer to the Jewish leaders as a whole or simply to Caiaphas, who instigated the cry for Jesus' death (John 11:49–53).

**19:12.** Although Pilate desired to set Jesus free, he was faced with the greatest threat to his position when the Jews claimed Pilate would be no friend of Caesar if he released one who claimed to be a king.

## Pilate Sentences Jesus to Death (19:13–16a)

**19:13.** When Pilate heard the threat, he knew he had been defeated. The interrogation of Jesus had taken place inside the palace. Jesus was sentenced, however, in the open court, a stone pavement, in front of the palace. Pilate brought Jesus out and seated himself on a raised platform from which he could view the crowd.

**19:14–16a.** According to the Gospel of John, the sentence took place at noon (the sixth hour) on the day of preparation for the Passover. Most authorities believe the Passover fell on the Sabbath that year. In preparation, work ceased, leaven was discarded, and the Passover lamb was slaughtered.

Although defeated, Pilate was not through. Normally in passing judgment, the crime of the individual was declared. In this case, Pilate presented Jesus to the Jews as their king. They again cried out for Jesus' crucifixion. Again taunting them, Pilate asked, "Shall I crucify your king?" The chief priests declared that Caesar was their only king. Even though Caesar was directly opposed to their religious belief, their hatred of Jesus led them to lie. Submitting to the will of the chief priests, Pilate handed Jesus over to the soldiers to be crucified.

Pilate attempted several times to put the responsibility for the fate of Jesus on the Jewish leaders. In the final analysis, Pilate had to make the decision for himself. In fact, all of us must decide for ourselves what we will do with Jesus. No one else can make that decision for us.

## The Crucifixion of Jesus (19:16b–22)

**19:16b–17.** It is interesting to note that the description of the actual act of crucifixion, as related by all the gospel writers, is almost limited to handing "him over to be crucified" (19:16). Crucifixion was so common that John likely felt no further description was necessary.

The four Roman soldiers commanded Jesus to carry his cross, which was the common practice. He carried only the crossbeam, for the vertical post was already in place. The place of crucifixion was outside the city wall in a public place where many people passed by. The place was called "the Skull," or Golgotha. The name likely arose because Calvary was located on a hill whose contour resembled a skull. The exact location is uncertain.

Crucifixion, a most cruel form of death, was reserved for those who had committed the most atrocious crimes against society, or against Rome. The prisoner's hands were nailed to the crossbeam. Then he was hoisted up to the vertical post, and the feet were nailed in place. Here the sinless Son of God was "lifted up" in fulfillment of his prophecy (12:32).

**19:19–22.** The common practice was to affix the name of the crime to the cross. In Jesus' case, to further annoy the chief priests, Pilate placed a sign reading, "Jesus of Nazareth, the King of the Jews." The sign was written in Hebrew (or Aramaic, NIV), the language of the Jews; in Latin, the language of the Romans; and in Greek, the world language. The chief priests objected. They asked Pilate to add that Jesus "claimed to be king of the Jews" (19:22b). Pilate forcefully denied the request.

## Jesus' Provision for His Mother (19:26–27)

Among the women who stood near the cross (19:25) was the mother of Jesus. Jesus spoke only to his mother and to "the disciple whom he loved." He addressed his mother as "woman," a respectful name, and told her to accept this disciple as a son who would bestow the love and care of a true son. He then told the disciple to accept Mary as his mother and provide for her the love and care a mother has a right to expect. From "that time on" this disciple's home became the home of Jesus' mother.

The question arises as to why Jesus designated this disciple for this responsibility rather than Jesus' half-brothers. It could have been that these "brethren" were not yet followers of Christ or were not financially able to assume the responsibility.

Jesus took time off from becoming the world's sacrifice for sinful people to provide for his mother. The care of aging parents becomes a challenge for many. Jesus sets a good example for us.

## The Death of Jesus: Mission Accomplished (19:28–30)

**19:28–29.** The humanity of Jesus is revealed in his cry, "I am thirsty." This cry also was a fulfillment of Psalm 69:21, "They . . . gave me vinegar for my thirst." The drink belonged to the soldiers and was diluted vinegar or cheap wine. The earlier casting of lots for Jesus' garments in John 19:24 was the fulfillment of Psalm 22:18.

**19:30.** After receiving the drink, Jesus shouted, "It is finished." The word "finished" means *accomplished*, referring to a task carried out to its ultimate completion. Christ had completed God's assignment for the redemption of humankind. He then voluntarily "gave up his spirit" (see also John 10:18).

## Jesus' Burial (19:31–42)

**19:31–37.** Because the next day was the Sabbath, the Jews wanted Jesus' legs broken that he might die and be taken from the cross. When the soldiers found Jesus was already dead, they did not break his bones. One soldier thrust a spear into his side (see Psalm 34:20; Zechariah 12:10).

**19:38–42.** Both Joseph of Arimathaea and Nicodemus, secret followers of Jesus and members of the Sanhedrin, combined their efforts to provide a proper burial for Jesus. Joseph gained permission from Pilate to take the body from the cross, and Nicodemus provided the mixture of myrrh and aloes for his body. They placed Christ's body in a nearby garden tomb.

## Focusing on the Meaning

*The inevitable question.* The inevitable question is, *How can the death of one man, two thousand years ago, atone for the sins of many?* The answer is beyond our ability to comprehend. God, however, does not ask us to understand it but to believe it. I certainly do not understand, after typing these lessons on my computer and clicking on "send now," how they get to the editor, but I believe it because I get a confirmation in return. The blind man whom Christ healed did not understand much if anything about Christ. Even so, he was quick to say, "One thing I do know. I was blind but now I see" (John 9:25). In the same manner, the saving power of the cross is validated by a changed life. Of this experience, Paul wrote: "Therefore, if anyone is in Christ, he is a new creation; the old has gone, the new has come" (2 Corinthians 5:17).

*Finishing the course.* When Jesus shouted, "It is finished" (John 19:30), he meant that he had accomplished his assigned task. Too many begin a ministry but quit somewhere along the way. Jesus becomes our example to be faithful unto death, to finish the course set before us.

*Living by faith.* Paul said, "I have been crucified with Christ . . . but Christ lives in me. The life I live in the body, I live by faith in the Son of God" (Galatians 2:20). By crucifixion Paul meant death to self and to self-will. Paul still lived by an active faith in Christ. First John 3:16 states that Christ laid down his life for us (meaning once and for all) and we are to lay down our lives (continually) for others. Christ, then, is not necessarily desiring that we die physically for him, but that we offer our "bodies as living sacrifices, holy and pleasing to God" (Romans 12:1).

# TEACHING PLANS

## Teaching Plan—Varied Learning Activities

### Connect with Life

1. Prior to class, enlist someone to share a five-minute testimony with the class related to his or her conversion experience. Encourage the person to share not only how and when he or she accepted Jesus as Savior but also how Jesus has provided help in daily life since then. After the testimony, point out to the class that they have just heard from one who is a modern-day product of an event that occurred

2000 years ago. Then read John 19:30 aloud, and invite someone to lead in prayer.

2. Briefly summarize John 18, using the comments in the *Study Guide* and in "Understanding the Context" in this *Teaching Guide*. Remind the class that the previous two lessons explained how Jesus prepared his disciples for the events that are revealed in John 18—21. Encourage them to keep the truths discovered in those lessons in mind.

## Guide Bible Study

3. Divide the class into groups of no more than six people each. Write the following assignment on the board or on a sheet of paper: Read John 19:1–16 and answer the following questions: *What flaws or weaknesses can be discovered in Pilate's argument with the religious leaders? Who had the most authority over Jesus—Pilate or the religious leaders? Why do you think so?*

4. After several minutes, invite each group to share answers. Comment as needed on John 19:1–16, using the information in this *Teaching Guide*. Then read John 19:11 aloud. Remind the class that Jesus gave his life willingly so that all people might have eternal life. Emphasize that Jesus stayed true to his mission in the midst of personal abuse and betrayal.

5. Prior to class, gather several newspapers and magazines. Get several rolls of masking tape and pairs of scissors as well. Ask each person in the class to find a partner. If there is an odd number, allow a group of three. Distribute some of the newspapers and magazines to each pair. Give each pair a roll of tape and pair of scissors. Ask each pair to search through the materials to find examples of abuse, betrayal, injustice, ridicule, and insult. The example may be a picture, story, or symbol. Instruct each pair to find as many as possible in a five-minute time span. As each pair works, encourage them to tape their examples to a focal wall as they discover them. Then, in a quick fashion, summarize all the examples you see on the wall. Point out to the class that Jesus experienced betrayal and insult in the highest degree and yet he willingly went through it for all of us.

6. Using the notes in the *Study Guide* on John 19:17–42, describe to the class the crucifixion, death, and burial of Jesus. Ask them to write down one-word descriptions of the emotional and physical pain that come to their mind as you tell the story. After you have finished, ask everyone to come at the same time and write anywhere on the board their words. You may need to provide several writing tools.

## Encourage Application

7. After everyone is back in their seats, encourage them to look at the board. Remind the class that Jesus willingly experienced all that is on the board and more because he loved them. Read John 19:28–30 aloud. Emphasize "It is finished" (19:30). Explain briefly the meaning of this sentence, using the comments in this *Teaching Guide*.

8. Give each person a 3" x 5" index card. Ask each person to write Jesus a thank-you note. After about two minutes, suggest that they place the notes in their Bibles at John 3:16. Close by encouraging them to read both their note and the verse each day this week.

## Teaching Plan—Lecture and Questions

## Connect with Life

1. Prior to class, write on the board the Main Idea of today's lesson as found in the *Study Guide* but leave a blank where the word "willingly" should have been placed.

2. Ask the class to read the small article, "Restorative Justice," in the *Study Guide*. Read John 19:30 aloud and tell the class that today the lesson is on the execution of Jesus. Emphasize that Jesus knew he was on his way to execution. Remind the class that not only did he not have chaplains to comfort him but also that some of his closest friends had betrayed and denied him.

## Guide Bible Study

3. Prior to class, write on separate pieces of construction paper the following headings: *Untroubled Spirit, Unshakeable Resolve, Unworthy Sentence, Undeniable Love, Unspeakable Grief.* Using tape or pins, attach them to the board or wall in a linear fashion as the class watches. Refer to these posters as you deal with each passage of Scripture.

4. Using the *Study Guide* notes on John 18:1–11 (refer to *Untroubled Spirit*), lecture to the class about the arrest of Jesus. Read 18:11 aloud, and stress the point that even in his arrest, Jesus *allowed* himself to be taken.

5. Make four columns on the board, and label them with these words: *Pilate, religious leaders, Peter, Jesus.* Have someone read John 18:12–27 aloud (refer to *Unshakeable Resolve*). Ask the class to identify at least one emotion or motive for each group or person. Write their responses as they call them out.

6. Enlist someone to read John 18:28—19:16 aloud (refer to *Unworthy Sentence*). Once again, call for emotions and motives for all columns except Peter's. (Perhaps ask for two or three about Jesus, Pilate, and the religious leaders this time.)

7. Read John 19:17–30 aloud (refer to *Undeniable Love*). Add to the columns again.

8. Using the notes in the *Study Guide* and in this *Teaching Guide* on John 19:31–42 (refer to *Unspeakable Grief*), summarize briefly the burial of Jesus Christ.

9. Lead the class in a discussion by using the questions in the *Study Guide.*

## Encourage Application

10. Read to the class John 18:11, 36; 19:11, 30. Then go to the board and fill in the blank in the Main Idea with the word *willingly.* Challenge the class to remember that Jesus *willingly* gave his life for all people. Summarize the comments under "Focusing on the Meaning" in this *Teaching Guide.*

11. Ask the class to bow their heads. Encourage each person to pray silently, thanking Jesus for dying for him or her and asking Jesus for the opportunity to share his or her testimony with another during the week.

## Focal Text

John 20:1–2, 11–29

## Background

John 20—21

## Main Idea

Jesus' resurrection appearances confirm his identity as God's Son and commission us to be his messengers to the world.

## Question to Explore

What does Jesus have yet to do for you to believe in him, serve him, and bear witness of him?

## Teaching Aim

To lead the class to confess their faith in Jesus as Lord

## UNIT FOUR

*Jesus' Glorious Triumph*

## Lesson Thirteen

# Seeing and Believing

## BIBLE COMMENTS

### Understanding the Context

In John 20:31, the author states the reason for writing his life and ministry of Christ: "that you may believe that Jesus is the Christ, and that believing you may have life in his name." Apart from the crucifixion and resurrection, neither of these desired results would be accomplished. Jesus, by his crucifixion, became our substitute, paying the price for our sins (1 Peter 3:18). He ransomed us by his death (Matthew 20:28), for "without the shedding of blood there is no forgiveness" (Hebrews 9:22). The death of Christ, however, would have been to no avail apart from Christ's resurrection. Paul said that "if Christ has not been raised, your faith is futile; you are still in your sins" (1 Corinthians 15:17).

No fact of history is more thoroughly validated than the resurrection of Jesus. The Bible records a number of post-resurrection appearances, the first five on the first day of his resurrection. Included are these appearances: (1) Mary Magdalene (John 20:11–18); (2) other women (Matt. 28:9–10); (3) two disciples on the road to Emmaus (Luke 24:13–32); (4) Peter (Luke 24:33–35); (5) the disciples, excluding Thomas (John 20:19–25); (6) the disciples,

143

including Thomas (John 20:26–31); (7) the disciples beside the Sea of Galilee (John 21:1–25); (8) more than 500 followers in Galilee (1 Corinthians 15:6); (9) the eleven disciples at the time of the giving of the Great Commission (Matt. 28:16–20); (10) James, the half-brother of Jesus (1 Cor. 15:7); (11) the disciples forty days after Jesus' resurrection (Luke 24:44–53; Acts 1:3–9); (12) Paul (1 Cor. 15:8).

## Interpreting the Scriptures

### The Empty Tomb (20:1–10)

**20:1–2.** Mary Magdalene was the first to arrive, early on Sunday morning. She found the stone rolled away from the entrance to the tomb. She was among the women who had stood near the cross (19:25).

What must have been Mary's thoughts as she observed the situation? She evidently thought the Jewish leaders or some robbers had taken Jesus' body away. Her immediate response was to tell Peter and John what she had seen. Peter, regardless of his denials, still seems to be the leader of the disciples.

**20:3–5.** Peter and "the other disciple" set out immediately for the tomb. "The other disciple" arrived first. He did not enter the tomb, though. When Peter arrived, consistent with his normal behavior he "went into the tomb" and observed the grave cloths lying there in an orderly fashion. Some believe that the linen headpiece and the body wrappings were lying as if Jesus' body had simply evaporated from the cloth. Others believe that the napkin, lying where Jesus' head would have been, was folded, as were the body wrappings. Regardless of these differences, the condition of the cloth dispels any thought that robbers had taken away his body, for they would not have taken the trouble to unwrap the body and neatly fold the cloth.

**20:6–9.** What Peter observed in the empty tomb created only a mystery, but "the other disciple," seeing the same thing as Peter, came to an entirely different conclusion. "He saw and believed." His belief came from seeing for himself the empty tomb. For him, that was evidence enough.

As an aside, John states that "they," the disciples, had not yet understood from the Scriptures that Jesus would be resurrected. An example of what John meant is the experience of the disciples on the road to Emmaus (Luke 24:25–27, 32).Even harder to understand is why the disciples did not recall what Jesus himself had said about his death and resurrection (see John 2:19–22; 16:22).

**20:10.** The two disciples returned to their homes, but there is no indication in the Gospel of John that they shared what they had seen with others. That Peter was still not convinced of the resurrection may explain his silence. Harder to understand is why the disciple who "saw and believed" did not share with others, unless he was waiting for further developments to validate his belief.

## Jesus Appears to Mary Magdalene (20:11–18)

**20:11–13.** Having determined to find the body of Jesus, Mary had returned to the tomb. At first she stood outside the tomb, crying because Jesus' body had been taken away. Then she looked inside the tomb and encountered two angels "seated where Jesus' body had been" (20:12). They asked her why she was crying. Her answer indicated that she had no insight into what had really happened (20:13).

**20:14–15.** Becoming aware that someone else was near the tomb, Mary turned to see who it was. She did not recognize Jesus but thought he was "the gardener." We can only speculate as to why Mary did not recognize Jesus. Was it because her mind was so intent on finding his body, or was it because she was blinded by her tears? Since she had no concept of Jesus' resurrection, she certainly would not have expected to see Jesus standing near her. She asked "the gardener" where he had taken him, believing "the gardener" would surely know about whom she was asking.

**20:16.** Mary came to the tomb seeking a dead body. Instead she became the first person to see the risen Lord. Her recognition of Jesus came when Jesus called her by name, Mary. She responded by calling Jesus "Rabboni," which means "Teacher." Mary's love, courage, and devotion, manifested in her standing near the cross, being first at the tomb, and returning to search for the body of Christ, brought her the honor of being the first to see the risen Lord.

**20:17–18.** The most natural way of interpreting verse 17 in the Greek text is *stop touching, holding onto, or clinging to me*. Thus, Jesus told Mary to stop doing what she was already doing. Most likely she had fallen at

Jesus' feet and embraced his legs. Why this admonition? Possibly it was that Jesus wanted no delay in delivering his message to the disciples. It may have been that Mary was clinging to a valued human relationship, but Jesus was now demanding the higher level of a totally spiritual relationship. Jesus' own explanation is the best interpretation: "Do not hold on to me, for I have not yet returned to my Father" (20:17).

Jesus then commanded Mary to tell "my brothers," that is, *my disciples*, that he was returning to the Father. Was Jesus referring to two ascensions? In attempting to coordinate the various accounts in the Scriptures, some suggest that the first ascension came between this conversation and his first appearance that evening with the disciples. Others hold to the view that Jesus was not talking about a specific date. He was in the process of ascending to the Father, the climax of which is described in Luke 24:50–53; Acts 1:6–11.

There is significance in Jesus' use of "my Father and your Father." Jesus' words indicate a difference between his personal relationship to the Father and the disciples' relationship to the Father. Jesus nevertheless identified himself with them.

Mary's first words to the disciples were, "I have seen the Lord!" Only with the personal appearance of Jesus later that day did the ten present believe, however.

### Jesus Appears to His Disciples, Except for Thomas (20:19–23)

**20:19–20.** The disciples evidently continued to meet in the upper room. On that first Easter evening, they were together, except for Thomas. The door was locked, for, in the absence of Jesus, they were more than ever fearful of the Jewish authorities. Jesus entered without opening the door.

What kind of body did Jesus have following his resurrection? He had told Mary to stop clinging to him. Later, he ate a piece of fish (Luke 24:41–42) and invited Thomas to touch his scars. We need to acknowledge that this question is beyond our ability to explain or comprehend.

Upon entering, Jesus gave the common Jewish greeting, "Peace be with you!" In this setting, however, the greeting held for the disciples a far more significant meaning. On seeing Jesus' hands and side, the confirmation of Jesus' identity, they received a peace that manifested itself in overwhelming joy as they beheld their risen Lord.

**20:21–23.** In his prayer to the Father, Jesus had said, "As you sent me into the world, I have sent them into the world" (17:18). Now Jesus commissioned the disciples with a similar statement. The earthly form of Jesus' ministry would be taken over by his followers. He "breathed on them and said 'Receive the Holy Spirit.'" This experience fulfilled John 7:39.

The words of Jesus in 20:23 must be interpreted in the light of all New Testament truth. Certainly Jesus was not giving the disciples in themselves the power to forgive sin. Rather, the reference was to their responsibility to proclaim the forgiving power of God in Christ and to warn that rejecting Christ would lead to condemnation.

## Jesus' Appears to the Disciples, Including Thomas (20:24–29)

**20:24–25.** Thomas's absence when Jesus first appeared to his disciples may be explained by Thomas's desire to bear his grief and disappointment in solitude, or he may have lost faith in Jesus' mission. Even when told by the other disciples that Jesus had risen, he still did not believe. He declared that he must both see and touch the scars on Jesus before believing. Remember two things about Thomas: First, he was a man of courage. When Jesus had said he was returning to Jerusalem, Thomas said, "Let us also go, that we may die with him" (John 11:16). Second, although called "Doubting Thomas," he doubted no more than his fellow disciples until they had seen the risen Lord (except for "the other disciple," 20:8).

**20:26–28.** A week later, with Thomas present, Jesus again appeared to the disciples. Knowing what Thomas had said, Jesus instructed him to reach out and touch his hands and side and to "stop doubting and believe." Likely, even without touching Jesus, he moved quickly from doubt to certainty as he cried out, "My Lord and my God!"

**20:29.** The emphasis of this verse is not on Thomas but rather on us. We have not had the privilege of seeing the risen Christ literally, as did Thomas, but we have, nevertheless, responded to him. Christ called us "blessed."

## Jesus Appears by the Sea (21:1–25)

**21:1–11.** Christ appeared again to the disciples beside the Sea of Tiberias (Galilee). Led by Peter, the seven had gone fishing. They needed to be busy rather than idle, and they also needed to eat. They did not recognize Christ on the shore. Nevertheless, at Christ's command, they cast their nets on the other side of the boat. After recognizing Jesus, there was still an uneasy feeling in his presence. He was the same Jesus whom they had followed for three years, and yet he was not the same. He now appeared in his glorified body. Jesus prepared a breakfast of bread and fish for them.

**21:12–19.** Jesus entered into a private conversation with Peter. He asked Peter three times—Peter had earlier denied him three times—whether Peter truly loved him. The first question was, "Do you truly love me more than these?" By "these" he likely referred to the other disciples. The three questions were rooted in Peter's assertion that he would be more faithful than all the other disciples (Matt. 26:33). To each assertion of love, Jesus commanded Peter to feed and care for his sheep. In that manner, Jesus affirmed Peter's apostleship in spite of his denials and commissioned him to shepherd his sheep.

Christ then began to describe the manner of Peter's death. In the years immediately following, Peter would move about as he pleased. After many years of faithful obedience to the commission of Christ, though, he would be crucified. Even in this, Peter would glorify God.

**21:20–23.** Peter seemed uncomfortable at this prediction. He turned and looked back at "the disciple whom Jesus loved" and asked, "What about him?" In essence, Jesus told Peter his business was to carry out his own ministry and leave the ministry of others to God.

**21:24–25.** The writer of the Gospel of John affirmed himself to be an eyewitness to the events described in it.

## Focusing on the Meaning

*Failing to recognize Christ.* Mary was not the last person to fail to recognize Christ's presence. Some are so caught up in their grief, sorrow, self-pity, or preoccupation with their everyday concerns that they fail to recognize the presence of Christ.

*Being found by Christ.* Mary did not find Christ. Christ found her. In all other religions, men and women seek their gods. Only in Christianity does God seek humankind.

*The resurrection body.* Even as we wonder about the nature of Christ's resurrection body, we may also be concerned about our own. Suffice it to believe "that when he appears, we shall be like him" (1 John 3:2).

*Stay close to fellow believers.* We know not the reason for Thomas's absence on that first Easter evening, but because of it, he missed seeing the risen Lord. Today, those who forsake the fellowship of believers, even in times of grief and disillusionment, cut themselves off from a great source of comfort, help, support, and spiritual blessing.

*Jesus' plan.* There is an oft told legend about Jesus' return to heaven to be questioned by the angel Gabriel as to how his ministry of reconciliation would be carried on in his absence. Jesus replied, "I have assigned the task to my disciples."

Gabriel then asked, "But what if they fail?"

Jesus replied, "Then I have no other plan."

The commission is to us all: "As the Father has sent me, I am sending you" (20:21). Christ is counting on us to carry his message to the ends of the earth, empowered by the Holy Spirit. We must not fail.

# TEACHING PLANS

## Teaching Plan—Varied Learning Activities

### Connect with Life

1. Prior to class draw a large question mark on one side of the board. On the other side, make two columns. One column should have the title, *Doubt.* One column should have the title, *Belief.*

2. Ask the class to think of some events in their lifetime that have become reality but at first hearing seemed impossible. Enlist a volunteer to write the events or things under the word, *Doubt.* Next lead the class to list elements that helped them move from doubt to belief. Ask the volunteer to write them under the word, *Belief.*

3. Read John 20:1–9 to the class. Point out that Mary, Peter, and "the other disciple" must have had many thoughts running through their heads as they saw the empty tomb. Doubts entered from every direction! State that today we are going to study two chapters that explain how the disciples moved from doubt to belief about the resurrection of Jesus Christ. Note that the class has listed on the board

certain elements they experienced before believing. The disciples also had their own roads to travel to belief. Pray and ask God's Spirit to guide the lesson today.

## Guide Bible Study

4. Summarize the unit of study to this point. Remind the class that Jesus gave us the supreme example of how a believer should act through his washing the disciples' feet (our example). Jesus taught them how to live out his commands and to know that they would never be alone through the work of the Holy Spirit (our resource). Jesus proved his love for the disciples by willingly dying on the cross for all people (our forgiveness). Now Jesus proved his authenticity through the resurrection and the resurrection appearances (our future).

5. Use the comments in the *Study Guide* and in this *Teaching Guide* to review and explain the events described in John 20:1–9. Refer to 20:9 and ask, *Why do you think the disciples had not understood about Jesus' resurrection from the dead?*

6. Divide the class into four groups. Tell them that we are going to examine four accounts of Jesus appearing to people after the crucifixion. Make the following assignments: a. John 20:10–17; b. John 20:18–23; c. John 20:24–31; and d. John 21:1–13. Give the following instructions: (1) Read the Scriptures assigned. (2) Identify how Jesus approached the people who were present. (3) Discuss why you think the individual or individuals responded as they did.

7. After about ten minutes, invite each group to give a report of some of their discoveries. As each group reports, use the information in the *Study Guide* and in this *Teaching Guide* to make additional comments about the resurrection appearances

8. Enlist someone to read John 21:15–19 aloud. Prior to class, write on construction paper the two different words for love used in these passages, with their definitions (see the *Study Guide*). Use masking tape to place them under the bottom of two chairs prior to the beginning of class. Using the comments in the *Study Guide,* explain to the class John 21:15–19. As you discuss the dialogue between Peter and Jesus, ask the appropriate person sitting in the chair to

find the construction paper and read the correct definition to the class. Point out that once Peter believed in the resurrection and recommitted his love for Jesus, he was never the same again!

## Encourage Application

9. Read to the class John 21:20–25. Ask the class to look at the two columns on the board again: *Doubt* and *Belief.* Remind them that their relationship with Christ is a personal matter. Note that when Peter asked about the other disciple, Jesus told him that was none of his concern. He was trying to teach Peter that his response should not be based on another's.

10. Restate the four appearances of the risen Jesus in this passage. As you say each, erase a small portion of the curved part of the question mark you placed on the board prior to class. (Jesus appeared to Mary Magdalene; Jesus appeared to the ten disciples; Jesus appeared to the disciples including Thomas; and Jesus appeared to the disciples by the sea.) The question mark should now look like an exclamation mark! Tell the class that if they personally believe, they too will follow Jesus. Read John 19:21 aloud, and send them forth!

## Teaching Plan—Lecture and Questions

### Connect with Life

1. Lead the class to find the small article in their *Study Guide* titled "Eloise Glass Cauthen: Never Too Young and Never Too Old to Be Sent." Encourage them to follow along as you summarize it or read it aloud. Then ask the class: *How would you describe the kind of relationship she had with Jesus?* As people talk, write key words from their responses on the board.

2. Connect step 1 with today's lesson by reading the Main Idea as given in the *Study Guide.* Point out that the resurrection of Jesus brings both meaning and purpose to our lives. Enlist a class member to pray.

## Guide Bible Study

3. Prior to class, on one side of the board write the following outline in the form of an arithmetic problem:

> The empty tomb
> \+ The appearance to Mary Magdalene
> \+ The appearance to the ten disciples
> \+ The appearance to the disciples including Thomas
> \+ The appearance by the sea
> _____
> **The testimony of changed lives!**

Draw attention to the outline. Tell the class that today's lesson is the last in unit four, on "Jesus' Glorious Triumph." Remind them that we have seen Jesus as Servant, Jesus promising to send the Spirit, Jesus as Savior, and now today, Jesus as our victorious Lord!

4. Refer to the questions in the *Study Guide*. Encourage the class to watch for answers to these questions and add insights to any answers they may already have arrived at.

5. Using the comments in the *Study Guide* and in this *Teaching Guide*, explain John 20—21. Follow the outline in the *Study Guide* and also put a check beside each section of the equation on the board as you share ideas on it.

6. Lead the class in a discussion of the lesson by calling for responses to questions 1–3 in the *Study Guide*. Affirm each answer while providing guidance to the truth of the lesson.

7. Ask each person to think of three things that are a reality in their world today that they would have considered impossible ten years ago. Ask for at least two responses. Explain to the class that we tend not to believe anything until we have personally experienced it. In other words, each person has to have proof.

## Encourage Application

8. Read the formula on the board again. Then lead a discussion of questions 4–5 in the *Study Guide*.

9. Tie the lesson into the unit by reminding the class that because Jesus achieved a glorious triumph over sin and death we can humbly serve each other, draw on the comfort and power of the Holy Spirit, willingly take up our cross daily, and point all people to the resurrection of Jesus as their only hope! Draw the attention of the class to the article in the *Study Guide* titled "Called and Commissioned." Ask the class to read it. Call for responses on items they could add to the list. After a time of response, lead in a prayer of commitment to believe in and follow the risen Christ, including sharing the good news of Jesus' resurrection.

# How to Order More Bible Study Materials

It's easy! Just fill in the following information. (Note: when the *Teaching Guide* is priced at $2.45, the *Teaching Guide* includes Bible comments for teachers.)
✤ = Texas specific

| Title of item | Price | Quantity | Cost |
|---|---|---|---|
| **This Issue:** | | | |
| *Gospel of John—Study Guide* | $1.95 | _____ | _____ |
| *Gospel of John—Large Print Study Guide* | $1.95 | _____ | _____ |
| *Gospel of John—Teaching Guide* | $2.45 | _____ | _____ |
| **Previous Issues Available:** | | | |
| *God's Message in the Old Testament—Study Guide* ✤ | $1.95 | _____ | _____ |
| *God's Message in the Old Testament—Teaching Guide* ✤ | $1.95 | _____ | _____ |
| *Genesis 12—50: Family Matters—Study Guide* | $1.95 | _____ | _____ |
| *Genesis 12—50: Family Matters—Large Print Study Guide* | $1.95 | _____ | _____ |
| *Genesis 12—50: Family Matters—Teaching Guide* | $2.45 | _____ | _____ |
| *Good News in the New Testament—Study Guide* ✤ | $1.95 | _____ | _____ |
| *Good News in the New Testament—Large Print Study Guide* ✤ | $1.95 | _____ | _____ |
| *Good News in the New Testament—Teaching Guide* ✤ | $2.45 | _____ | _____ |
| *Isaiah and Jeremiah—Study Guide* | $1.95 | _____ | _____ |
| *Isaiah and Jeremiah—Large Print Study Guide* | $1.95 | _____ | _____ |
| *Isaiah and Jeremiah—Teaching Guide* | $2.45 | _____ | _____ |
| *Matthew: Jesus As the Fulfillment of God's Promises— Study Guide* ✤ | $1.95 | _____ | _____ |
| *Matthew: Jesus As the Fulfillment of God's Promises— Large Print Study Guide* ✤ | $1.95 | _____ | _____ |
| *Matthew: Jesus As the Fulfillment of God's Promises— Teaching Guide* ✤ | $2.45 | _____ | _____ |
| *Jesus in the Gospel of Mark—Study Guide* | $1.95 | _____ | _____ |
| *Jesus in the Gospel of Mark—Large Print Study Guide* | $1.95 | _____ | _____ |
| *Jesus in the Gospel of Mark—Teaching Guide* | $2.45 | _____ | _____ |
| *Acts: Sharing God's Good News with Everyone—Study Guide* ✤ | $1.95 | _____ | _____ |
| *Acts: Sharing God's Good News with Everyone — Teaching Guide* ✤ | $1.95 | _____ | _____ |
| *Romans: Good News for a Troubled World—Study Guide* ✤ | $1.95 | _____ | _____ |
| *Romans: Good News for a Troubled World—Teaching Guide* ✤ | $1.95 | _____ | _____ |
| *1 Corinthians—Study Guide* | $1.95 | _____ | _____ |
| *1 Corinthians—Large Print Study Guide* | $1.95 | _____ | _____ |
| *1 Corinthians—Teaching Guide* | $2.45 | _____ | _____ |
| *Galatians: By Grace Through Faith, and Ephesians: God's Plan and Our Response—Study Guide* ✤ | $1.95 | _____ | _____ |
| *Galatians: By Grace Through Faith, and Ephesians: God's Plan and Our Response—Large Print Study Guide* ✤ | $1.95 | _____ | _____ |
| *Galatians: By Grace Through Faith, and Ephesians: God's Plan and Our Response—Teaching Guide* ✤ | $2.45 | _____ | _____ |
| *Hebrews and James—Study Guide* | $1.95 | _____ | _____ |
| *Hebrews and James—Large Print Study Guide* | $1.95 | _____ | _____ |
| *Hebrews and James—Teaching Guide* | $2.45 | _____ | _____ |
| **Coming for use beginning June 2003** | | | |
| *Amos, Hosea, Micah—Study Guide* | $1.95 | _____ | _____ |
| *Amos, Hosea, Micah—Large Print Study Guide* | $1.95 | _____ | _____ |
| *Amos, Hosea, Micah—Teaching Guide* | $2.45 | _____ | _____ |

## Beliefs Important to Baptists

| | | | |
|---|---|---|---|
| *Who in the World Are Baptists, Anyway?* (one lesson) | $ .45 | _____ | _____ |
| *Who in the World Are Baptists, Anyway?—Teacher's Edition* | $ .55 | _____ | _____ |
| *Beliefs Important to Baptists: I* (four lessons) | $1.35 | _____ | _____ |
| *Beliefs Important to Baptists: I—Teacher's Edition* | $1.75 | _____ | _____ |
| *Beliefs Important to Baptists: II* (four lessons) | $1.35 | _____ | _____ |
| *Beliefs Important to Baptists: II—Teacher's Edition* | $1.75 | _____ | _____ |
| *Beliefs Important to Baptists: III* (four lessons) | $1.35 | _____ | _____ |
| *Beliefs Important to Baptists: III—Teacher's Edition* | $1.75 | _____ | _____ |
| *Beliefs Important to Baptists—Study Guide*<br>(one-volume edition; includes all lessons) | $2.35 | _____ | _____ |
| *Beliefs Important to Baptists—Teaching Guide*<br>(one-volume edition; includes all lessons) | $1.95 | _____ | _____ |

---

*Charges for standard shipping service:

| | |
|---|---|
| Subtotal up to $20.00 | $3.95 |
| Subtotal $20.01—$50.00 | $4.95 |
| Subtotal $50.01—$100.00 | 10% of subtotal |
| Subtotal $100.01 and up | 8% of subtotal |

Please allow three weeks for standard delivery. For express shipping service: Call 1-866-249-1799 for information on additional charges.

Subtotal _____

Shipping* _____

TOTAL _____

Number of FREE copies of *Brief Basics for Texas Baptists* needed for leading adult Sunday School department periods _____

---

Your name                          Phone

---

Your church

---

Mailing address

---

City                          State          Zip code

**MAIL** this form with your check for the total amount to
BAPTISTWAY PRESS
Baptist General Convention of Texas
333 North Washington
Dallas, TX 75246-1798
(Make checks to "Baptist Executive Board.")

OR, **FAX** your order anytime to: 214-828-5187, and we will bill you.

OR, **CALL** your order toll-free: 1-866-249-1799 (8:30 a.m.-5:00 p.m., M-F), and we will bill you.

OR, **E-MAIL** your order to our internet e-mail address: baptistway@bgct.org, and we will bill you.

We look forward to receiving your order! Thank you!